ESCAPING THE
NIGHTMARE
Tragedy to Glory

Written by
Richard Kiser

Published 2018. Written by Richard Kiser.
Edited by Deb Patterson and Kelly Kiser.

Cover Photography and Design by Aidan Kiser
Cover Art Production by Bob Schamerhorn of Infinity Graphics

ISBN 978-1984242143

PREFACE

A few years ago I shared my testimony about how God helped me through a two year bout with Post-traumatic stress disorder (PTSD). This was a result of being shot in a hunting accident. After that testimony, a friend who is a professional counselor suggested I share my story in book form. She informed me that there are many clinically written self help books but there are very few, if any, written from a personal standpoint and from personal experiences.

This book is my story of what I put my family through during my hard times. It is a story of how I was in denial about having a problem, and finally, it is a story about how God revealed Himself to me during my most difficult times. First, through His Word and secondly, through His faithfulness and His blessings. It is also a story about how God can take a tragedy and nightmare and turn it around to use it to bring Glory to Him.

My prayer is that God will reveal Himself through my story and encourage you to put more trust in Him.

Thanks to my wife Esther for supporting me through these years of denial and hardship and for her patience and understanding during a difficult time. Also thanks to Lin and Vicky Bown for encouraging me to complete this book. Most of all, thanks to our Veterans who have suffered untold hardship by making sacrifices and protecting our freedom. There are untold thousands who still return home from serving our country in combat and suffer from PTSD. It is my desire that this book will bring more awareness to the dangers and heartaches of PTSD, as well as understanding to those who suffer from it, and how God can help us through it.

Special thanks to my daughter-in-law, Kelly, and my grand daughter, Katelyn, for their help in editing. Thanks to my three sons, Rick, Tony and Danny for help in recalling some of the incidents. Thanks to Deb Patterson for her hard work in proof and editing. Thanks to my wife, Esther for her prayer and patience during my times of PTSD and for her support during the writing of this book

CONTENTS

INTRODUCTION

I have always loved the outdoors. I have wonderful childhood memories of walking down to the Roanoke River that flowed through our neighborhood to fish for bluegills, carp, and anything else I might catch. When I was 13, my Uncle Chuck took me squirrel hunting. I felt like a real man with that .22 single-shot rifle in my hands. I was actually going to go out and pursue a wild animal to bring home to eat. He lectured me on making a safe and clean shot. We did not want to risk wounding any living creature, ever. I was nearly overwhelmed with excitement as well as the new sense of responsibility with which I had been entrusted. I did not want to let my uncle down.

Even though that first hunt resulted in no game, at least for me, it sparked a passion in me that to this day has never been extinguished. As years passed and I became a man, that love for the outdoors never waned. I realized that there were two passions in my life that would never die: music and the outdoors—especially hunting and fishing.

This book is not about hunting. It is about daily life, family, our passions, tragedy, and most of all, how our relationship with our God can make a difference in how we deal with it all.

—Richard Kiser

Chapter 1
THE THRILL OF THE HUNT

In 1968 I returned from my tour in the military, ready and anxious to be a husband and start a family. I also decided that it was time to rediscover my love for the outdoors. I found myself reading all of the outdoor publications I could find, which began to whet my appetite to be back out in the woods. My dad gave me a model 1917 Springfield .30-06 rifle that he bought through mail order. I can still remember the smell of cosmoline that it was coated with to preserve it for decades of non-use. It was heavy and bulky and a little hard to handle, but then it was built for combat, not for hunting. The first few times I fired it at the range, it brought back memories of my days at the firing range in the Army.

That first fall season, after practicing with a few boxes of ammo, I decided I was ready to go out to hunt for whitetail deer. Every deer hunter has a special memory from that very first hunting season, and mine is etched permanently in my mind.

It was the last day of my first deer season and so far, I had not even seen a deer. Back then, the last day was "doe day," which meant that it was legal to harvest does on that day. I had walked at least a mile back into the national forest, and I sat down to wait for a big buck to walk by.

Sure enough, after an hour or so I heard something. I

turned toward the sound and looked down a long ravine—what we Southerners call a "hollow." Out of nowhere, there appeared an 8-point buck, walking straight toward me. I turned, pointed my rifle toward him, and waited for that perfect shot. Well, it never came. He walked behind some brush and magically just disappeared. I could not believe or understand how he had just vanished! I will never forget, however, that trembling excitement, which I later learned was called "Buck Fever." It seemed like forever before my heart rate would slow down.

After another half hour or so, I decided to head to the car to meet my dad and Barry, my other hunting buddy, for lunch. I had to tell them my story. I began to walk up the ridge and the moment I came into a clear cut, I stepped on a twig. Not twenty yards in front of me, two giant bucks stood up and looked at me with a startled look on their faces. They immediately turned and bolted, and I began firing as fast as I could operate the bold action of that old rifle.

After shooting at least four rounds and missing each time, my heart was so shaken that I just turned and headed for the car. As I walked along and reloaded, I scared up a buck that was bedded down. Again I fired three shots and again, I missed all three times. By the time I got to the car, I was so disheartened that I was about ready to give up and go home. As I told my dad and Barry my story, all they could do was laugh, although I failed to see the humor in it. I was so rattled, I couldn't even eat my lunch. I went back into the woods and left them there at the car, still laughing.

At that point things got really crazy. I had not walked a half mile across the hollow when not seventy-five yards away, there stood a doe, broadside. This time I would take my time and do it right.

The back end of the deer was barely behind some brush, but I knew it was a safe shot so I dropped down on one knee, took aim, and fired. I saw her fall, but she got up and ran, so I quickly bolted the rifle and fired again. She fell, then got up and ran again, so for the third time I fired. The third shot did the trick; she was down for good.

I hurried over to claim my harvest and was elated to find my deer lying there. After hearing all the shooting, Dad and Barry had headed toward me and when they arrived, I was standing over my prize. I was excited almost to the point of tears; I had killed my first deer, and this winter we would have some fine venison.

Dad began to help me field dress the deer. (Field dressing is opening the cavity of the deer to remove the internal organs, which speeds up the cooling of the meat and helps to prevent spoilage.) While we were preparing the deer to be dragged out of the woods, Barry looked over and said, "What's that over there?" We looked, and not thirty yards away was another dead doe. My heart sank as it dawned on me that I had shot another one. Upon further exploration, we realized that in my inexperience and excitement, I had taken three deer. What I had thought was the doe falling and getting back up turned out to be three different deer. Thankfully, neither of the others had filled their tags, so we were able to check in all three deer.

I learned a lot of lessons that first year that were not mentioned in Outdoor Life magazine. The biggest lesson I learned was that I still had a lot to learn! Yet even with the mistakes made that fall, I will never forget that first season of deer hunting. I had no idea of the stories and memories I would be creating over the next few decades, not to mention the lifelong friendships that would be made after days spent in the woods and in deer camps.

The next year, I decided to try my hand at spring gobbler hunting. I read all I could find about how to call and identify a male turkey, which is called a gobbler or tom. It sounded pretty simple: be in the woods before daylight and listen for that thunderous gobble-gobble-gobble, then use a cedar box call and make a sound like a hen turkey. The gobbler would fly off the roost toward the sound of the hen and there he would be, an easy target. At least that's the way my Outdoor Life magazine said it was supposed to happen.

The funny thing was that the first time I went out to try my hand at spring turkey hunting, it happened pretty much just like that. I went into the woods right at daylight and listened. I heard an old tom gobbling on the roost and had to stop myself from running in his direction. The excitement was almost overwhelming.

I walked to a spot that I figured was within seventy-five yards of where he was and sat down against a large tree. I took my Lynch box call and began to slide the top across the box, creating a keouk-keouk sound. The gobbler immediately responded and I heard him fly down off his roost. Once again, he let out a gobble-gobble-gobble. As I sat there and began to shake with excitement, I slid the top of the call against the box again: keouk-keouk-keouk. Immediately the turkey sounded again, only this time I could hear him walking in the leaves. I knew he was coming to me, and I tried talking to stay calm as he drew closer. I raised the shotgun and rested my hand on my knee. Within seconds, I could see his white head working its way through the small scrubs and brush. With my thumb, I flipped the safety off the twelve-gauge shotgun and waited. "Keep calm and don't blow this," I kept telling myself as I sat there trembling with excitement. In order for me to get a clean kill shot, I knew he would need to be within about forty yards.

The difficult part about getting that close to a wild turkey is that their vision is excellent. They can actually see you blink an eye at that distance, so I could not move. After a couple of minutes, which felt more like an hour, he stopped and raised his head high to see if he could see the hen he was after. That's when I took my shot. He went down flopping and bouncing, and I knew I had gotten him. My first time out, I had killed a twenty-three-pound turkey with a 9½-inch beard. I thought, this is way too easy.

Count that as another lesson I would learn about hunting. Lesson being harvesting wild game can often appear to be easy, as it was with that first gobbler, but in most cases it takes hours of preparation and days of pursuit, often in extreme weather conditions.

I soon discovered that every trip into the woods in pursuit of wild game would be a lesson about nature, about our Creator, and often about life itself. These would be lessons to pass on to my children and grandchildren. After all, isn't that part of God's master plan for us anyway, to share what we learn with future generations? In the decades to come, I would learn many more valuable lessons.

Chapter 2

GOBBLE GOBBLE

Seven years of hunting seasons had passed, and it was Easter of 1976. This was a special time for our family. Every year my wife, Esther, would get up early and hide Easter baskets, leaving clues all over the house for our young sons, Rick, Tony, and Danny. When they awakened, it was like Christmas morning. They would run around the house laughing and screaming, searching for their plunder.

I, however, had another type of hunt on my mind. The next morning was the opening day of spring gobbler season, which had become one of my favorite times of the year. I was excited about the possibility of calling in and harvesting another wild turkey. The weather forecast for Monday was excellent, a cool, clear, cloudless spring morning, the kind of morning that makes music in the forests. I had already prepared my shotgun, my camo clothes, and a couple different kinds of turkey calls. I was pretty sure sleep would not be easy because of the excitement. Finally, it was time to get the kids to bed and go to sleep myself because morning was going to come quickly.

The next day, my alarm went off at 5:00 a.m. As I crawled out of bed, I could hear the quiet idle of my dad's Datsun pickup truck in the driveway. He would always pull in the driveway and never get out, just sit there and sip coffee and wait for me. He knew I was up and would be out soon. In the kitchen, I could hear my own coffee maker brewing, and I could smell it as I got ready and began to come alive. I'm usually not a morning person, but that changes during hunting season.

With my backpack in hand—complete with my box turkey call, a thermos of coffee, some shotgun shells, gloves, and a camo head net—and my shotgun case in the other hand, I quietly slipped out the door, being careful not to awaken the rest of the family. I said good morning to Dad as I jumped into the truck, and he gave me his usual good morning grunt.

The ride to the Jefferson National Forest near Eagle Rock was about thirty-five miles, and there were usually very few words spoken between my dad and me. Neither of us were really talkers that early in the morning, but somehow we always seemed to communicate without speaking a word. About the only discussion we had that morning was deciding which direction we would go when we parked the truck at the foot of Patterson Mountain. I chose to take a logging road which went east, and Dad chose to head west toward the base of the mountain. I noticed a white Ford pickup truck parked at the spot where we were going to begin our hunt. I silently wondered if it was just one person or a couple of hunters.

It was still dark, just predawn, and you could barely see a shimmer of red to the eastern sky as the sun was just beginning to show a ray of ambient light. There was a beautiful quietness in the forest that morning, except for the occasional sound of a bird singing its wake-up song. In the distance, I heard a lone tom turkey as he let out a loud gobble-gobble-gobble to greet the new day. I felt my heart race as I realized his call came from the direction I would be heading. For a moment I again wondered if this other hunter who was parked here could be in the area where I was going. I decided to not worry about it and focus on the hunt.

As I uncased my old single-shot 12 gauge shotgun and grabbed a few number five shot shells and my backpack, I wished Dad good luck and headed out on the logging road. Although I had about a half-mile hike ahead of me, I didn't bother to bring a flashlight because the sun was beginning to light the way for me.

After about twenty minutes of walking, stopping, listening, then walking again, I thought I was getting within a few hundred yards of a turkey who had let out a few gobbles from his roost, telling the hens he was there. I could also hear a few crows as they began to sound their morning greetings.

The usual routine for spring gobbler season is to use some sort of call device like a box call or slate call, or even a diaphragm call, which is placed in the mouth and blown. They are all used to imitate a hen turkey in hopes of luring a male turkey during the spring mating season. It is one of the most exciting hunting methods, especially when you are out in the woods and start to hear that big gobbler answering your call and getting closer. When you see the white head of a turkey and see his tail feathers fan

11

out into a full strut position ... wow. There is no greater rush.

This spring morning was invigorating, as the darkness was slowly overcome by the morning sun and the forest began to come alive. In the eastern sky, I could see crimson as the sun began to make its daily appearance. I heard a few squirrels as they were scampering out of the trees in search of their morning meal. While walking on the logging road, I stopped as a whitetail deer crashed through the woods, startled by my appearance. He was snorting his alarm as he ran and I just smiled, thinking, I hope I see you in the fall.

As I reached the area where I was going to set up, I removed my backpack and loaded my shotgun. I sat at the base of a large oak tree, took out the box call, and made a few yelps. After about three minutes and no response I tried again with a soft keouk-keouk-keouk. I thought to myself, you sound pretty good, old boy, and sure enough I heard a distant gobble-gobble-gobble. I turned toward the direction of the sound and let out a few more yelps. This time, I got an immediate response, and I began to get excited.

I could tell that the turkey was getting closer. I didn't want to call too much, so I just sat quietly and waited for several minutes before making a few more yelps. I heard the gobbler respond, but he was not getting any closer. I tried again, this time a little more aggressively; he answered immediately but still was not moving. This went on for probably half an hour.

I heard a few more turkeys in different directions, but none of them were coming my way. The most aggressive one sounded like he was a half mile or so behind me. The gobbler that I was trying to call seemed to be ignoring me, and I figured he had probably met up with a hen on the way. The sun was getting pretty high since it was about 7:15 a.m., and I decided there was no point in sitting there any longer. The time was right for me to relocate and try to call in another bird.

I stood up and donned my backpack. With my caller in one hand and shotgun in the other, I set out in the direction of the distant gobbler. It was about two hundred yards back to the logging road and I figured that the other turkey was several hundred yards down the road and on the other side. I would take a few steps, then stop to look and listen, hoping once more to hear that gobbler reveal his whereabouts. Although I had not heard him for twenty minutes or so, I still knew I was headed in the right direction.

All along the way, I just drank in the beauty of that cool, clear spring morning. I thought about what a gift it was from our Creator to paint such a beautiful picture as a hardwood forest. I savored every detail—the woods, the birds, and the wildlife with which He had so perfectly decorated this part of our world—and I wondered how anyone could ever question the existence of God. I had planned a full week's vacation to be out here, and I felt blessed. Later in the day, I planned to drive a few miles down to a clear stream that had been freshly stocked with trout. It felt so good to be alive, and I was enjoying every minute of it.

As I walked along that morning, enjoying the peaceful surroundings, I had no idea that within a few minutes my life would be changed forever.

Chapter 3
"DEAR GOD!"

After crossing the logging road I walked for about a hundred yards across the top of a hardwood ridge. The woods were very open at this point, and I knew I would need to walk for a bit to get out of the open area. It was around 7:30 by then and legal hunting time didn't end until noon, so I still had plenty of time. Sometimes I actually prefer to hunt gobblers later in the morning; it seems easier to call and get a response at that time rather than right after daylight. As I walked quietly through the woods, heading toward the area where I had heard the turkey, I had my shotgun over my shoulder and my camo head net rolled up over my hat.

All of a sudden, I heard a shotgun blast from the right, and instantly my ear began ringing. I felt an enormous pain in the right side of the top of my head, as if someone had just hit me with a baseball bat. I started to fall from the force of the impact as it spun me around. As I was falling, I saw a hunter with his shotgun positioned as if he had just fired it. It was then that I realized I had just been shot.

I let out a scream and thought, this is a dream; it's not happening to me. Everything seemed to be moving in slow motion as I fell face down to the ground. I heard footsteps rapidly moving toward me and for an instant I thought, dear God, please don't let him shoot me again.

I was afraid to move, but as he approached he placed his shotgun against a tree. All he could say was, "What have I done?"

I raised my head and felt blood flowing from my head over my face and ears. I then got a close look at his gun, an imported over/under shotgun and rifle with a scope. When I saw the scope my next thought was, I have just been shot in the head with a high-powered rifle, and this is where I am going to die. For just a second I experienced an unbelievable peace, but it was quickly followed by sadness as I remembered my wife, Esther, and my sons, Rick Jr., Tony, and Danny.

I was sure I was about to leave my family and for a moment I felt their grief. Then, as I thought of their names, my mind began to reason again. I started to think that if my brain was still working, then maybe the top of my head was not totally blown off—but I was still afraid to put my hand up there to feel.

Once I became aware that I was totally conscious, the shock began to overrule the pain and I became numb all over. I remember asking, "The Man" (to protect the family of the shooter I will refer to him here as "The Man") if my skull was still intact or if it was blown away. He was also going into shock by this time, and he repeated, "My God, what have I done?" He was trembling and becoming panic-stricken. He kept saying, "I didn't mean to shoot you. I thought I saw a turkey." He finally told me that my head looked bloody but okay. I pulled out a bandana and slowly placed my hand on my head to slow the bleeding.

The Man was getting more hysterical by the moment. I asked him to help me stand. As I rose to my feet, I felt a sharp pain in my right arm and coldness on my shirtsleeve. The sleeve was bloody, and when I tore it open, I saw that I had been shot in that arm. Noticing that my chest also felt cool and wet, I ripped open my shirt to see that my T-shirt was bloody. I then realized that I had at least three shots in me. (I was later told that it was number two buckshot from three-inch magnum shells. Number two buckshot is almost the size of a 22-caliber bullet per shot.)

I realized the shot in my chest was in close proximity to my heart, and fear started to sweep over me again. As this nightmare continued to unfold, I kept thinking, I cannot believe this is happening to me. I'm a happily married father of three boys, I have a job, I love my Lord—this can't happen to me. The pain in my arm shot through me again, and I knew that I had to get out of there and get help.

The Man was still just standing and staring. I asked him to go get help, and he said he would not leave me. For some strange reason at that time he said, "I didn't mean to shoot you, I really thought you were a turkey." He continued, "I can't believe I didn't kill you. I have killed a bear with this gun and this shot." I can't imagine why he felt that it was the appropriate time to tell me this other than the fact that he was in shock.

He eventually helped me up and picked up my shotgun as I picked up my turkey call, hat, and head net that was rolled up on top of my hat. The hat was blown to pieces and the head net was full of holes from the shot. If The Man had aimed just half an inch lower, I would still be lying there. It's amazing how quickly different thoughts race through your head during a trauma like that.

I was brought back to reality as he helped me start walking and asked if anyone was out there with me. I told him that my dad was on the other side of the main logging road. The Man started to panic again, afraid that my father would kill him when we got to the truck. I tried to reassure him that my dad was a cool-headed man and nothing would happen. Again, he said something strange: "I know if someone brought my son to me and said that he had just shot my son, I would kill him." Again I tried to reassure him that my dad would be okay and that we just needed to get out of there.

By then some of the pain had subsided, but I was feeling a bit weak and nauseous from shock and blood loss. I walked for a few minutes before I had to stop and rest. I sat on a tree stump, trembling from shock and disbelief. Once more I pleaded with The Man to go get help and come back for me. Again he said, "I am not leaving you."

I began to pray, saying, "God, please help me get out of here on my own strength. Please give me strength to make it out." The Man asked what I was doing and I replied, "I'm a Christian. I believe in God and I was praying for strength to walk." Then I stood up and began walking. I was cold, I was weak, and I was numb, but I just walked, one step at a time. We walked for about fifteen minutes, saying very little. The only time The Man spoke it was to say how sorry he was for shooting me and that he was afraid my dad was going to shoot him.

When we reached the final bend, we were in sight of the truck and I saw my dad standing there. I cannot even begin to fathom the horror he must have experienced when he saw me soaked with blood and being half carried by someone. I immediately said, "I have been shot but I think I'm okay." The Man said in a trembling voice, "I shot your boy, but I didn't mean to." Dad stared at him with a blank, questioning look. He just said "Damn!" and shook his head. He then looked me over and helped me into the truck. I told him if we could get to the main road, maybe he could use his CB radio to call for help.

I had never seen my dad drive so fast on an old logging dirt road. He never spoke a word, but he would look over at me every few minutes and shake his head as I leaned back against the seat. By then, the blood was dried on my face and my head was just a dull ache.

When we reached the main highway, Dad found a trucker on the CB radio. I had never in my life seen fear in my dad's eyes or heard it in his voice until I heard him talking to that truck driver on the CB. He said, "My boy has been shot by a hunter and we are heading south on route 220 towards Fincastle. Have the rescue squad ready to meet us there to take him to the hospital."

When we reached the town of Fincastle, the rescue

squad was waiting for us. I asked for some water but the EMT only allowed me a few sips. I didn't understand why he wouldn't let me drink more, and he explained that they could not risk it, not knowing the extent of my injuries. They laid me down on the gurney and began the twenty-five-mile trip to the hospital. I asked Dad to go on to my house and tell Esther what had happened, but first tell her I was okay. I knew if he told her that, she would believe it and come to the hospital immediately.

As I lay in the ambulance the EMT began to check my vitals and prepare me for the emergency room at Community Hospital in Roanoke. When we arrived and they rolled me in, I remembered that my mother-in-law worked in the laundry room at that hospital. I was still feeling a bit lonely and scared, so I asked the nurse to go get her. Before they got me cleaned up, my mother-in-law arrived. All she could do was stand there and cry and pat the top of my hand. She stayed by my side until my wife got to the hospital.

I learned later that my dad stayed at my home to watch my sons. I did not dare tell the boys what had happened. The funny part is what happened when my boys realized that Mom and Dad were not there and they were being watched by Grandpa. Even though they had just gotten out of bed, they each went to the refrigerator and got out their Easter candy, knowing that Grandpa would never say a word. Each of my three sons ate an entire chocolate Easter bunny for breakfast that day.

After the wounds had been cleaned and dressed, and

countless X-rays had been taken to verify the location of the three buckshot pellets, I asked the doctor if he was going to remove them. He laughed, saying that I had been watching too many movies, and he told me that the shot would not be removed. He assured me that scar tissue would grow around the pellets and they would never move. Somehow that was not a comforting thought to me, but to this day, the buckshot pellets are still in my body. After a few hours of observation, the doctors told me I would be allowed to go home that night, but to stay in bed for a few days to recover from the blood loss. Exhausted, I was happy to be able to go home—and even happier just to be alive.

Chapter 4
TWO VICTIMS

The day after I returned home from the hospital, I was visited by two Virginia game wardens, Officers Jim Nance and Dennis Mullins. At first, I was surprised and even a little intimidated to see them, but they let me know right from the start that they were there only to investigate the accident and gather as much information as possible. I had to lie there and totally recap the entire incident as they asked questions and took notes. I had never experienced anything like that, and I remember being astonished when they asked me if I thought the shooting was not an accident. I told them of course I thought it was an accident; I didn't even know the man.

The last question they asked was even stranger to me. They asked if I wanted to press charges against him. I emphatically responded, "No! I don't want to press charges. It should not have happened, but it was an accident." Back then, in a hunting accident, no charges would be filed unless the victim decided to press charges. Since then the laws have changed, and now the State automatically charges the shooter with a minimum of reckless handling of a firearm.

The game wardens then told me that they were going to visit The Man and question him as well. When they asked if there was anything else I wanted to say, I told them yes. "I know the reason I am still alive. I am a

Christian and I know God has spared my life." They just reminded me that I was lucky to be alive and wished me well.

My physical recovery time was only a few weeks, and I was starting to feel somewhat like my former self again. I was confident about my progress, but I was not ready to even think about going back into the woods. I did, however, feel a deep, compelling need to go visit The Man. I wanted to find some sort of closure and to let him know that I did not intend to prosecute or bring a lawsuit against him. I just felt this need to relieve him of that worry.

About three weeks after the accident, I went to his home, which was in a little town called Eagle Rock, Virginia. The first meeting was very emotional for both of us. I drove to his house and walked what felt like a mile to his door, when in reality it was only a few feet. I was trembling as I knocked on the door. What would I say? What would he say? Would I be welcome? Would he talk to me?

He lived with his wife in a small log cabin in the woods. When I stepped into his living room, I saw trophy mounts of bear and deer, as well as dozens of wild turkey fans and beards. My first thought was wow, this guy has killed more game than I have ever even seen in my lifetime. He asked me how I was, and I could tell he was very uneasy and nervous because I was in his home. These were awkward moments, but I felt we both needed the closure.

He began to apologize and express how badly he felt about the accident. He told me that he would pay all of the hospital bills even though he didn't have much money. He said he would do what was needed to pay the bills, and I explained to him that I didn't come here for that. Instead, I wanted to assure him that I had no intention of suing him and that my insurance had already taken care of the hospital bills.

With tears in his eyes, he again started to apologize for the accident. His wife then came into the room and asked me if I would like some coffee or a soda. She was a very sweet lady in her mid-fifties and very much a mother at heart. The first thing she asked me was about my family and how many children I had. I told her I had three sons, ages three, five, and seven. With that, she began to cry and blot her tears with her apron as she walked out of the room.

A few minutes later she came in with something to drink and a piece of cake, looking at me again with mournful eyes. She turned to her husband and said, "You almost left these boys without a father," then left the room as she began to cry again.

The atmosphere was so somber. With another tearful look, The Man asked if there was anything he could do. He told me he was a gunsmith and he could give me a hunting gun or anything I wanted. He seemed to feel such a need to try to make amends by giving me a gift. In his despair, he was trying to earn some sort of release from the guilt and shame he felt for making such a devastating mistake.

That day, I learned that an accident such as this can result in two victims. Both the shooter and the victim will bear a scar that will never be healed. Even if the accident was a result of poor judgment or even what some would call neglect, it was still an accident. Any retribution that I might try to claim would only have deepened the scars for both of us. Instead, I took the opportunity to remind The Man that he was forgiven and owed me nothing in return. I also told him that Jesus Christ offers us even greater mercy and forgiveness for our sins that is also undeserved and cannot be earned.

I left him that day and dropped by a few weeks later for one more visit, just to let him know that I was alright. His wife tearfully thanked me for letting them know that I was going to be okay, and wished me and my family well. As I walked from their house to my car, I could see her waving with one hand as she blotted a tear with that same apron.

During that visit I learned that they had a grown son who had just lost his job at the local sawmill. He had supposedly been laid off because of lack of work, but his mom and dad said he was dismissed because of the hunting accident. News of the accident had spread through the little town and apparently stirred up too much emotion and controversy at the mill. I felt really bad about that as I left. It seemed so unfair that a young man who had nothing to do with the accident would have to bear the responsibility.

As far as I know, The Man continued to hunt. I saw his truck parked at the same spot one time a few years later. I often wondered what went through his mind as he walked that same trail alone. I never saw him again. As I pondered everything that had happened to both our families, I was reminded that life isn't always fair, and that God tells us in Matthew 5 that the rain falls on the just as well as the unjust.

Chapter 5
"WHAT IS HAPPENING TO ME?"

Over the next couple months I began to think my life was going to get back to normal. I was trying to forget the accident and nearly convinced myself that it was working.

In late June, my wife and I took our sons to visit her sister and husband in Pennsylvania. We left right after work on Friday night and drove my white Ford Pinto station wagon to Mechanicsburg, Pennsylvania. My wife was going to spend a few days up there with her sister, Ava, while I returned home to spend a few days alone. I was looking forward to some peace and quiet with no wife and no kids for four days.

A couple of significant events occurred while we were in Pennsylvania. The first one was an unexpected blessing—our family gained a new member. Shortly after we arrived, we ended up in a discussion about owning a dog. It just so happened that Esther's sister had a friend who had a new litter of black Labrador Retrievers. With one simple phone call, we became the proud owners of a beautiful black Lab we named Sheba. At only eight weeks old, she was so fragile and cute. She fit right in the console of our little station wagon with her head rested on my lap. How cool, I thought; I had found a new friend.

The second big thing that happened on that trip took me completely by surprise—and shook me to my core.

On Saturday afternoon, my brother-in-law John mentioned that there was a stock car race just a couple of miles away that evening. Auto racing had always been an adrenalin rush for me. I loved the sound, the smell of high-octane racing fuel, and the excitement that hovered over a race track, whether it was a drag strip or dirt track. John and I decided to take a guys' night out, and within an hour we were walking up to the ticket counter of the raceway.

We shuffled through the crowd and found seats in the grandstands just out of the fourth turn, about halfway up the bleachers where we could see everything. We began watching the "heat" races, during which a few cars would race at a time to qualify for positions in the main race. Even though the main race had not yet started, everyone there seemed to share the same rush of pure excitement.

As the cars sped around and around the track, my own mind took a turn that I never saw coming. For some reason that I did not understand, I began to feel very uneasy. I started feeling threatened and scared, and I had no idea why. Ashamed to say anything to John, I simply excused myself and told him I was going to the concession stand for a soda. I could not seem to get out of that grandstand fast enough. I found myself running past the concession stands and past the restrooms to an area under the bleachers where I could be alone.

I began to cry uncontrollably. I was scared and trembling, and I could not fathom what was going on. "What is wrong with me?" I kept asking myself. "God, what is going on? I was having a great time—why am I here crying like this?" Never had I experienced such strong emotions for a reason I couldn't even identify.

After a few minutes, I went to the concession stand and bought a couple of sodas and hot dogs, then returned to my seat. At that point, the feature race had started and the sound pierced both my ears and my entire chest in a constant vibration from the thirty or so cars that were totaling over 15,000 horsepower.

Just like before, I began to feel closed in. As I watched those drivers push their cars to the very edge of losing control on that dirt track, I again felt tears starting to flow. Luckily, there was so much noise and excitement from the crowd that no one was paying any attention to me. I wanted to tell John to take me home, but I guess the macho in me just had to overrule my common sense.

I sat there for the next hour or so, looking for reasons to go back to the concession stands to try to get away from the crowd and the noise, if only for a moment. I could not imagine what was wrong. What could possibly make a thirty-year-old father of three cry like a baby at an auto race? Even the thought of having to ask such a question made me angry. I realized that something was going on in my mind over which I had absolutely no control, and I wrestled with the shame of it all. I'm a man, and this is a man's sport, I told myself. Get a grip on yourself, Rich.

After struggling for a while, I came up with some

reason to convince John that we needed to leave. He asked no questions; we just got in the car and headed back home. When we arrived, Esther suspected something was wrong. Making up some lame excuse, I convinced her that I was okay, so she dropped it. I had no idea that what was going on in my mind was about to control my life for the next few years—and change it forever.

The next day was Sunday, the day I'd planned to drive back home and spend a few days alone. At first I was still pretty excited at the thought of being home alone for almost a week. Then, just as I was about to leave, it hit me—I would be all alone, no wife, no kids, in a quiet house. I suddenly had a sickening feeling of emptiness and fear. Within an instant, I became aware that I was afraid to go home alone. This is nonsense, I thought. I'm a grown man. I have spent many nights alone at home and even some away from home. What is going on with me?

I decided to take our new pup Sheba to keep me company on the return trip, thinking that might help. After lots of goodbyes, I drove off, Sheba in her newfound little perch in the console with her head in my lap. I could not believe how safe and secure I felt with an eight-week-old puppy in my lap, but at that point, I didn't care—I was not alone.

Sheba and I endured the next week until John and Ava brought my family back home. It wasn't until months later that I told Esther about the sinking feelings and fear of being alone that I had experienced that week.

Chapter 6

NOT OUT OF THE WOODS YET

At last, my favorite time of year was about to roll around—fall and hunting season. It was my first post-accident hunting season, but at that point I wasn't giving any thought to the possibilities of flashbacks or fear of hunting. I just wanted to get out to the woods.

I took every spare moment I had to do pre-season scouting. Many afternoons, I would leave work and head back to the national forest, to scout for deer sign, such as tracks, bedding spots, and other indications that deer were present. However, I did not consider going back to the place where I was shot.

Archery season turned out to be fruitless for me. I never even got a shot at a deer but I loved the fall season, the beautiful colors that God so perfectly painted in the forest once a year.

At last, it was time. It was the Sunday before opening day of deer season, and I was so excited. When I went to bed, all I could see each time I closed my eyes was a nice buck walking into gun range. Like each year before, it seemed impossible to go to sleep the night before opening day of deer season. Where would I go? Would I move the wrong way and scare my trophy away? Would I miss the shot? These and a hundred more questions kept jogging through my head in sequence, preventing sleep.

Bright and early, the alarm jarred me awake—it was

time. Jumping back into the familiar routine, I made a pot of coffee, ate some cereal, and slipped quietly out the door when Dad's old blue Datsun pulled into the driveway. Time to head back to the woods. It was opening day and I felt so lucky to get to go deer hunting.

After our thirty-five-mile ride, Dad dropped me off near the old railroad bed, which was next to a natural watering hole. I had a fifteen-minute walk through this hollow to reach my deer stand. It was daylight by then, and I was feeling confident.

Then, out of nowhere, a terrible feeling swept over my body. All at once I remembered that I was in the woods again with hunters who had guns, and I became terrified. That hopeless and helpless feeling that I had experienced at the race track in Pennsylvania was back. I started to look around, imagining there was a hunter with a gun behind every tree. Even though I was wearing blaze orange, I felt vulnerable. Within minutes I was so scared that I found myself lying face down on the forest floor trembling, wailing, and crying uncontrollably. Once again, I had no control of my emotions and felt like I was going to die.

I later wondered what any hunter would have thought if he had come upon a grown man in blaze orange and camo lying face down in the woods and sobbing like a baby. What a wild picture that must have been.

After a few minutes of lying there crying, it was like I had a reality check. I said to myself, "Either get up and go home, or get up and go hunting." I stood up, dusted off my clothes, and proceeded to walk to my stand.

After that experience, I did alright for the rest of that hunting season until Thanksgiving Day. I was near the top of a mountain, maybe seventy-five yards off the logging road that twisted to the top of the mountain. I was sitting at the base of a large tree overlooking a ravine that I knew was well traveled by deer. At around 7:00 a.m. I heard a four-wheel-drive truck climbing the mountain, and I could hear the hunters talking.

When I heard the truck stop and a door slam, my mind began to betray me again. I found myself huddling up into a fetal position with my gun at my feet. I could actually feel that hunter focusing on me with the crosshairs of his rifle. I had my eyes closed and I was crying as I prayed, "Dear God, please don't let him shoot me." Then, as if an angel sat down beside me, I felt comfortable again and began to sit up and enjoy the view as the sun was slowly burning the frost off the leaves on the far side of the ridge. Later that morning, I watched a doe and two fawns as they played in the sunshine on that same ridge, totally oblivious to the hunters who were less than three hundred yards from them.

I did not get a deer that day, but I was reminded that God was still with me, protecting me. For the rest of the season, I had no more problems with the fear of being shot. At that point, it was seven months after the hunting accident and I still did not know that I was beginning to go through something that would have been diagnosed as Post-Traumatic Stress Disorder. I just thought I was being a bit too emotional, which frustrated me. Deep down inside, I felt that I should have been tougher about it all.

I remember talking about being shot a few times to certain men whose initial reaction was, "That so-and-so better be glad he didn't shoot at me, or he would be a dead man. I would have shot back." I was often amused and sometimes angered at the "tough guy" attitude that some men so boldly expressed. I never said it, but I usually thought, "Brother, when that hot piece of lead splits your scalp open and you feel like you just got hit with a baseball bat, you don't know what you'd do, so don't give me that line."

The other common response was, "Did you sue him for all he was worth? You should be a rich man from that one." It is still scary to me to see the way some people, even Christians (that word Christian is supposed to mean Christ-like), are out to find personal gain from a tragedy or accident. The fact is, I will never forget every detail of that April morning, but neither will The Man who pulled the trigger.

Things seemed to return to normal for the rest of that year, and we enjoyed a great Thanksgiving and Christmas season with our sons. During that season of reflection, I was especially thankful and grateful to be alive. I expressed that both at home with my family and in church when given an opportunity. Still, the battle wasn't over. I didn't know it then, but many more challenges were to come.

Chapter 7

VISIONS OF TERROR

It was later that same winter that things really started to deteriorate for me emotionally. The first episode was a horrific nightmare.

We lived in a modest Cape Cod house in Roanoke. Our three sons slept upstairs in two bedrooms, and my wife and I slept in the main level bedroom. One night I had a vivid dream that someone stood outside our bedroom window, which was just off the front porch, and fired a handgun at me through the window. I clearly heard the gun blast and felt glass fly all over the bed. It was so real that I came up out of the bed, screaming, and nearly knocked Esther out of bed. I was crying and sweating and trembling from something that I clearly thought was real.

Esther held me close and kept whispering, "It's alright, it's going to be alright. It was only a dream." How could I be so weak that I had to find comfort and security in my wife's arms? What was wrong with me? Why couldn't I just accept this as a bad dream and go back to sleep? Unfortunately, these questions were not to be answered right away.

Some weeks later I was awakened again by a sound in the house. I just lay there at first, trembling, trying to figure out if I was dreaming or not. Esther was still asleep, and I tried to go back to sleep. It's only my imagination,

I thought. Then I heard it again.

This time I told myself, "You are the man here; get up and check it out." I got a shotgun from the closet and loaded it. I walked upstairs to check on the boys first, and they were all sound asleep. Then I returned to the main level and continued down to check the basement. When I turned on the basement light and looked around, everything appeared to be fine. I wondered if I had heard anything or if I had imagined it all. I finally returned to my room, unloaded the shotgun, and got back in bed. As I lay there, again I started wondering what in the world could be wrong with me. After a half hour or so, I fell back asleep.

As the weeks passed, I began to notice that I was getting more paranoid about life in general. I started to worry and think "what if?" about everything. Sometimes I would think up an entire episode of some sort of tragedy, something happening to one of my kids or my wife. I would visualize it to the point of getting upset or depressed.

One Saturday night that spring, Esther was trying to get the boys to bed and they were being "boys." She had to go upstairs and threaten them a few times to get them to settle down. At one point she saw Tony standing by his bedroom window, but we were not aware that he had been talking through the window to a neighbor kid outside.

All of a sudden I heard a bang, thump, thump, and a

scream. Esther ran out of the bathroom downstairs and said, "Dear God, Tony has fallen out of the window!" Since I had heard the sounds and the yelling, my mind painted the entire picture; I saw it all happen. I ran outside, and Esther ran upstairs. She found Tony in bed, while I found the neighbor's kid outside. He had banged on the door and run screaming as a prank.

Esther came downstairs, relieved that nothing bad had happened. In my mind, I still saw my son falling out of the window, and I could not recover from it. I could not grasp the fact that it was an innocent prank. I mourned Tony's death for days. Nothing was able to bring me back to reality—not prayer, not talking, nothing would work. Every night when I went to bed, I relived my son falling, heard the screams, and saw him hit the ground. It was then that I started realizing that I had a serious problem.

I also constantly battled depression. I had all the symptoms, but refused to believe it. I experienced loss of appetite, I felt bad practically all the time, and I had no energy. My wife stayed by my side through all of this, exercising all the patience she could, and she never complained. Some of my other family members, however, were quick to diagnose what was wrong with me and even offered some of what they called "nerve pills." They told me that was exactly what I needed.

During this entire time I was working as a service technician for a business machine company, and I never lost any work time because of my problems. In fact, I tried to hide the problems by getting more involved in my job. Sometimes it would hit me even during work, though.

One day I had been working in Christiansburg, Virginia, and I had just gotten into my car to head home. Just as I put the key in my ignition, I heard the horrible sound of tires screeching and then a child screaming and crying. Before I even turned to see what happened, because of what I had heard, I visualized the child getting hit by a car.

When I looked, I immediately saw that the child had fallen out of the back of a station wagon at the stop light, and it just scared her. She was not hurt at all, and she ran crying and climbed back into the car. The problem for me, however, was that my mind reacted in a similar way to the incident with my son. I visualized the child getting hit by a car, and a wave of emotion came over me. I sat there and could not stop crying.

A passerby tried to console me and then had to call my wife. Someone had to bring Esther all the way to Christiansburg to drive me home. Each day, it felt more and more like I was losing control. Even so, I was convinced that I could wait it out and work things out on my own. I felt like my mind was locked up in a prison, but I was still sure that I could escape.

Chapter 8

BEAMS OF LIGHT

I still stayed very active in our church during all of this, serving as a Sunday school teacher and Royal Ranger leader. My church involvement is one thing that did help to keep me focused and was probably more therapeutic than I realized.

One Sunday after church, I was outside joking with some friends when a close friend of ours, Bootsie Moore, walked up to me. Bootsie always seemed to be very perceptive, and she told me she wanted to say something. I sort of joked around with her, but she looked me straight in the eyes and said, "You hide your hurt so well, but God really wants to help you. " How could she possibly know? I thought. I have never told anyone what I have been feeling. I wondered if God truly was using her as a messenger to let me know He wanted to help me. Nah, I thought, she was just being motherly, that's all.

The funny thing was, that simple phrase haunted me for weeks. I thought, did God love me enough to send someone to give me a simple message of hope? I pondered it often but was not yet ready to confront my issues. I still wanted to deny that there was a problem.

A few months later my boss called me in and told me I needed to go to Connecticut for a new machine launch and training. I would fly to La Guardia and then commute by train to Stamford, Connecticut. At first, I was excited to take another business trip and break up my life's routine with a week away from home.

I received my plane ticket and as the time to leave approached, I started feeling that sinking sensation again. I was afraid to leave home. When I went to bed at night, I began to visualize the plane crashing. One day I even went to my boss's office and told him I was having some family problems (figuring this was a safe way to hide the real problem) and asked if he could send someone else. My boss informed me that I needed to make this trip, and he did it in such a way that I knew I had better plan to go.

The Sunday afternoon that I was to leave I felt fear, loneliness, and guilt. I was ashamed to tell my wife that I was afraid the plane was going to crash. I felt foolish for even thinking it, yet I was still convinced. As I boarded the plane, I wore sunglasses because I was trying to hide my tears.

I looked out the window of the plane at Esther and my three sons waving at me. I felt as if it were the last time I would see them, and I was even mourning my death for them. I wanted to unfasten that seat belt and run through the plane and out the door screaming, "No! No! I cannot go! I don't want to leave my family!" Somehow I managed to stay there, my eyes fixed on my family as the plane began to rev up its engines. I kept thinking, this is not fair. I should not have to die like this. As the plane taxied to the runway and prepared for takeoff, I whispered a prayer. "God if I have to go like this, I'm ready, but I ask you for protection and to spare my life."

After all of my worrying, we arrived safely in New York City. I was then faced with the commute to Stamford, which consisted of an hour-long train ride and then a limo ride. By the time I got to the hotel in Stamford, I was exhausted.

In order to save hotel expenses, my company would always make us share our room with another person. Whenever I went on these training trips, I never knew who my roommate would be or what kind of person he would be. This time, God decided to send another one of His nuggets of blessing, reminding me that He was there.

When I checked in, my roommate for the week was already checked in. I walked in the room and set my bags down on the other empty bed, then introduced myself. I am beginning to feel somewhat human again, I thought, even though I was so homesick already. My roommate shook hands and told me his name. I asked if he was hungry and he was, so we agreed to walk downtown and find a restaurant.

While walking, we were exchanging small talk and out of the blue he said, "Richard, you might as well know right up front that I'm not like a lot of the service reps that come up here. I am a born-again Christian and I don't go for the drinking and partying that often goes on." I responded, "Praise God!"

In all my years of traveling up there, no one had ever said anything like that to me, and this time it was the one thing I needed to hear. We had a nice dinner and talked about our families, our hometowns, and our jobs. I could not wait to get back to the hotel to call Esther and tell her about the special little gift God had sent me for this trip.

For the next week, we spent our days in class learning the new equipment, and we spent the evenings sharing God's Word with each other and talking about the things of the Lord. As I look back on those days, I am reminded that even at the darkest times in our life, if we look and try to recognize it, we are made aware that God sends little beams of light just to let us know that He still shines. Sometimes we don't even recognize it until later, but it's always there.

Chapter 9

IMPRISONED BY FEAR

It was approaching two years since the hunting accident, and the nightmares were occurring more frequently. I had just about accepted the fear and worry as a way of life, thinking it was something I would have to live with. When things were going pretty good, I worried even more. I would wake up every morning expecting a tragedy at any moment that would upset my life again. I expected that something would happen to my wife, one of my children, my parents, or me. I was beginning to realize that I was living in a prison—not a literal prison, but something much worse. I was living in the prison of my own mind, and I did not even know who had the key anymore.

It's sad, yet funny how others can often see the bars that imprison us, and yet sometimes we refuse to see them. For some reason, be it pride or stubbornness, we deny that they exist.

By that time, there were a lot of people who recognized that I was having a problem. Some family members were suggesting that I get professional counseling, while others were suggesting that I visit a doctor to get something to help me sleep more soundly. Everyone meant well, but no one knew a thing about what I was suffering from, Post-Traumatic Stress Disorder. The fact is, I didn't even know about it. All I knew was that the prison walls of fear, depression, nightmares, and panic attacks were closing in more and more every day.

Through it all, the person who showed the most patience and understanding was my wife. She never criticized; she did not even get upset with me when I told her that very next hunting season that I planned to go back into the woods. She actually encouraged me to go back.

As time went on, I felt that I was becoming more and more detached from my own emotions. I felt like I was totally out of control, but my pride kept telling me that everything was okay. After all, I thought, I'm a grown man, I can handle anything. I am a father of three little boys. I have to be strong. I'm a Christian. I should be able to take whatever life puts before me. I'm a smart guy, I can reason this out. There must have been a hundred excuses I was able to think of to justify the fact that I did not need help. I just knew that all I needed was a little more time and that things would work out on their own. I figured that I was still a young man and time was on my side. If I could just tough it out, I would be a better man for it. Unfortunately, I was mistaken.

In May of 1978, we went on a family vacation at my aunt and uncle's house down on the Rappahannock River near the mouth of the Chesapeake Bay. My sons loved to go there and ride the boat with Uncle Wayne and go "crabbing" out on the dock just outside his house. There was always something fun to do there.

We decided that we were going to spend a few days at Virginia Beach, but we would start our vacation with a weekend at my uncle's place. The drive to the coast was an exciting trip because Rick, Tony, and Dan were trying to out-talk each other as they planned what they were going to do at the beach and at Uncle Wayne's.

When we arrived, it was a beautiful Saturday afternoon. Uncle Wayne and Aunt Betty were planning a cookout and when the boys got out of the car, they went running in every direction, trying to figure out what activity to do first. My cousin was also there with her kids, so it promised to be a fun afternoon.

Wayne always seemed to have some new "toy" that enticed the kid in all of us, and this time was no different. He had just bought a new three-wheeler ATV. Even I could not wait to climb on that machine and ride around the grassy fields that surrounded their house. We were all taking turns riding and having so much fun. I took each of my sons for a ride, showing off my skill and trying to impress them.

After a little while, Rick decided that he was old enough to go for a ride on his own, without Dad. After all, he was nearly nine years old, much too old to have to ride behind Dad. I decided maybe he was old enough, so he climbed on the little Honda ATV and I showed him all of the controls. "Here is the gas, you push it with your thumb," I told him. "Here is the brake. Now don't drive it too fast; just go out into the field and back." The smile on Rick's face was an image that I never wanted to forget.

47

Little did I know that it would soon be replaced with a different image, one that would leave another scar in my mind.

As Rick made the second round out into the field, he turned to drive back toward all of us standing by the split-rail fence and waiting on him to pull up and stop. He was driving in our direction, but he was not slowing down. It was then that I recognized a petrified look on his face and saw that his hand was locked on the throttle. I immediately began to have a helpless, sick feeling as I saw him drive past me directly into the split-rail fence without even slowing down.

Thankfully, the front wheel hit the center rail and almost stopped the vehicle, but the top rail caught Rick in the chest, clotheslining him off of the ATV. I stood there dumbfounded as I watched my son get killed. At least, that is what my eyes told my brain. In reality, Rick was only knocked off the three-wheeler and his chest and chin got a little bruised. He got up, crying and shaken and very embarrassed. On the other hand, I had just witnessed my son die as he drove through a fence while I stood helplessly only inches away.

I ran and picked him up and even though he was very much alive, I was feeling this deep, sickening pain and guilt. I should have known better, I thought. He was too young to be on that thing. How could a responsible father make such a bad judgment call? I could not get the picture out of my mind. As the minutes passed, I began to feel worse. I was nauseous and feeling weak. I was so thankful that my son was not badly injured, yet deep inside I was mourning his loss. My mind was lying to my heart, and I was believing it.

I held Rick and talked to him, and I would not let him out of my sight for the rest of that evening. When we went to bed that night, sleep would not come. I lay there looking at the ceiling, reliving every moment of that accident. I wanted to go to sleep, but I was afraid that the same picture would come back as a nightmare. It truly was like being in a prison, being able to go from one room to another, but knowing I was still locked up.

The next day was no better. By then, Rick was back to normal and ready to go to the beach with his family. Esther was packing and the boys were excited about going to Virginia Beach. I was struggling to get out of bed, still feeling sick. The horrific picture from the day before was still vivid in my mind. I was experiencing that all-too-familiar lonely, helpless feeling as I fought back the tears.

All I wanted to do was get in the car and go back to the only safe sanctuary I knew of; I wanted to go home. How would I explain this to the boys? How would I explain it to my wife? I could not even understand what I was feeling myself. Now there was another fragment of guilt to deal with—I was going to have to cancel my family's vacation because I could not cope with a problem.

Sometimes it seems that when one thing goes wrong, it is so easy to go back and count all the other bad things that have happened. I had a growing total of bad things in my life, and depression joined the list of emotions that I was going through. The family was so disappointed when they received the news that we had to go home. I don't recall what I said to them, but I'm sure that out of sheer guilt, I promised them all something to make them feel better and to help me feel justified.

The drive home was not happy or pleasurable. I had three unhappy boys and a worried wife. It was on the trip home that Esther finally decided to express her concern, trying her best to be encouraging. She was never critical, but in a delicate way she let me know that maybe it was time to consider getting some help. By now I was beginning to realize that my problem was not just "my problem"—it was affecting my entire family.

My kids had no idea what was going on. They just knew that sometimes "Daddy would get upset," but Esther was experiencing the gradual loss of her husband. She was trying to be strong for both of us, covering up her own concerns to maintain a smile for our sons. She was being so strong and so unselfish.

What an emotional nightmare it must be to watch someone you love waste away in a prison of fear and anguish. I know there must have been times that she was feeling helpless, yet had to remain strong for the sake of giving the family some sort of structure and security. When I look back on it now, I'm not sure she didn't suffer more than I did.

Chapter 10
ACCEPTANCE

There were many times during those two years after the accident that life seemed to be going along just fine. Normally, a family is able to savor and enjoy times like that, as they make special memories that will last forever. My job was going well, the kids were fine, and the bills were being paid, but there was still something wrong. There was a cloud in the back of my mind that hovered over me, preventing me from completely relaxing and enjoying the good times.

I fought hard not to worry, trying not to think too much. When I started thinking, that's when I would get into trouble. Even during these stable times I often got a little paranoid, expecting any moment to hear some tragic news or experience something terrible that would upset our lives again.

Still, I tried to live my life as though everything was fine and normal, and most of the time, it was. I thought that maybe I would be alright. Maybe the nightmares were over. Maybe I was going to get over all of this after all. But then, in August of 1978, I experienced a major setback that caused me to realize that, in fact, I was not okay.

I was a Royal Ranger leader at our church. The Royal Rangers organization was founded by the Assemblies of God as a ministry to boys, similar to the Boy Scouts of

America. Skip Salmon, the district commander of our district of Royal Rangers and also one of my closest friends, invited me to go to a "Ranger Pow Wow" in North Carolina. Skip was their guest speaker, and we were to be special guests at the Pow Wow. I was going to take my guitar and play a few songs around the campfire at night. When we got there, we were treated like VIPs. The food was delicious, and I was having a great time. I never expected that one of their rituals for waking up the camp would severely set me back.

One of the elite groups in Royal Rangers is called the Frontiersmen Camping Fraternity, or FCF. It was created for the most advanced of the Ranger boys, and also for the leaders. In the FCF the men and boys would take on the personas of men in frontier days. Most of them would wear costumes of that era, such as buckskins and leathers, and they would shoot black powder rifles and learn to throw tomahawks.

Around 7:00 a.m. one morning, the FCF members staged a mock Indian raid, running through the camp, firing their flintlock rifles, and yelling. The flintlock rifles were not loaded; they only had tissue paper packed in the muzzle so the powder would ignite and make a loud "bang" but when they went off, it was as loud as a shotgun or rifle.

I was sound asleep in one of the tents, all snuggled in my sleeping bag, when one of the men stood outside my tent and fired his flintlock. I came out of my sleeping bag in a screaming terror and began to ball up in a fetal position and cry uncontrollably. Well, needless to say, Skip had to drive me home right away. The man who fired the flintlock felt terrible about what happened, but there was no way he could have known what was going on with me or how I would react. The ride home from North Carolina was a long one. I talked with Skip on the way back and began to recap the past two years with him.

I have to say, that event was the one thing that caused me to finally accept the fact that I needed help and I needed it badly. I felt a little relieved, because I believed I had at last reached the pinnacle of this long ordeal. I felt like I had a new revelation, and I couldn't wait to get home to my wife and boys. My problem was not solved, but at least I knew I was going to get help and start on a road to recovery.

At long last, I was able to admit to myself that I was indeed suffering from Post-Traumatic Stress Disorder. It went by other names as well—"Delayed Stress Syndrome" was one, and the terms "shell shock" and "combat stress reaction" were often used in times of war. Now, the proper name is Post-Traumatic Stress Disorder, or PTSD.

During the Vietnam War era, there were many veterans diagnosed with this disorder. Some began to show symptoms immediately when they returned to the States; others would not experience problems until years later. Many of them resorted to drug or alcohol abuse to try to overcome the problems, and some got counseling. Many of these veterans would overcome the disorder through counseling and medical treatment, but some are still battling it decades later.

Although it is an issue often identified with veterans, PTSD is not confined to that group. It is a disorder that attacks people of all ages and walks of life, and it is not confined to gender. There are men and women of all ages who experience PTSD as a result of trauma in their lives. The first step in overcoming PTSD or any other psychological problem is recognizing that there is, in fact, a problem.

That is where I found myself, nearly two and a half years after the hunting accident. I was finally able to accept that I had a real problem, and I was ready to do whatever I could to find help.

Chapter 11
FIRST TASTE OF FREEDOM

The first step on my road to recovery was a conversation with a trusted friend—my pastor, Glen Strickland. After church one Sunday morning I asked him if we could meet as soon as possible. I really think he was expecting me to come to him for help, and he agreed to meet me the next day.

I went into his office at Faith Assembly of God Church that Monday and for about an hour, I poured my heart out to Pastor Strickland, telling him all that I had gone through and of the fear that was tormenting my life. He sat there and listened to everything I had to say, but it was almost as if he already knew what I had been going through—and he even had an answer for me. He informed me that just as Satan had attacked Job and God would not allow him to take Job's life, he had attacked my body and had not succeeded in taking my life. Therefore, he was going after the next most vulnerable target: my mind. If Satan could succeed in stealing a person's mind, their body would eventually succumb as well.

Pastor Strickland opened his Bible and turned it to 2 Timothy 1:7 and read it to me: "For God has not given us a spirit of fear but of power and of love and of a sound mind" (NKJV). He then took out a three-by-five index card and wrote the Scripture on the card for me.

Next he told me, "I have an assignment for you. I

55

want you to carry this card with you everywhere you go. Whenever you begin to feel fear or have a panic attack, take out this card and read this Scripture aloud." That's when my pastor began to remind me of the power of God's Word. He reminded me that when Jesus was being tempted on the mount by Satan, Jesus would answer every temptation with "It is written" and then He would quote God's Word. Pastor Strickland truly felt that the Scripture would help me to overcome this problem just as it helped Jesus overcome the temptations from Satan.

I left there that day feeling encouraged. The simple counseling that my pastor had given me sounded so simple, yet was so powerful.

I carried that card around with me everywhere I went. When I went to work, it was in my shirt pocket. When I got home from work and changed clothes, it went in the next pocket. I guarded it as if it were a shield covering my heart.

Every night before I went to bed, I would take the card out and read it aloud; it was my lifeline. I treasured this simple little card because it was a promise, a declaration from God: "For God has not given me a spirit of fear, but of power and of love and of a sound mind." God wanted me to have a sound mind. God wanted me to have power. HE really wanted that for me. What an awesome promise. I was going to believe this promise no matter what.

Every morning when I got in my car and started to drive, out would come the card and I would read it aloud, repeating it over and over and over again. Sometimes I would say it for five to ten minutes at a time. If I started getting nervous or my mind began to wander into an area that might cause me to worry, out came the card. If I were to go back and try to count the times that I recited this particular passage of Scripture, I could only estimate that it would be in the thousands.

I went to bed quoting 2 Timothy 1:7. I woke up quoting it. I even thanked God for giving me a sound mind, knowing that I was about to be healed. As days turned into weeks, I began to feel different; there was a new feeling that was beginning to dominate my thoughts. The constant nightmares diminished, and the panic attacks seemed to stop altogether. I was beginning to experience restful sleep. It was after a few full nights of sleep that it suddenly occurred to me—it had been days since I had been awakened by a nightmare.

I was feeling different during the day too. My work felt easier and I found myself smiling more often. I even had a renewed desire to reacquaint myself with an old friend I had abandoned over the previous two years— my guitar. Music had been a major part of my life in the first few years of my marriage, yet somehow I had lost all interest in it. As I began to play again, I felt the passion for music returning. I would often come in from work, pick up my guitar, and begin to pour out my heart through the strings. There was, once again, a melody that was alive and resonating throughout the house.

The changes were so subtle that it took a while for

me to realize that God had healed me. It almost came as a shock—I am healed! I am free! No longer would I have to live in a prison of fear. I was amazed that I had experienced a true miracle, and yet my mind filled with many questions. What's next? Did it really happen? Will the nightmares return? Where do I go from here? Do I start to testify of God's healing power right away? Esther was excitedly sharing my joy—she had her husband back!

I could not wait to meet with Pastor Strickland again and declare my healing. When I talked with him, he rejoiced with me and we had a prayer of thanksgiving. He also encouraged me to not be afraid to boldly testify of my healing, reminding me that I would become even stronger through my testimony. I looked forward to going to church and sharing my testimony openly for the first time.

I recalled the statement Bootsie Moore had made a year before: "You hide your hurt so well." At that time I was overwhelmed that she had the ability to see through me, but I never forgot what she said. Now I could testify that I no longer needed to hide my feelings or emotions. Now I was free.

Chapter 12

HOPE AND HEALING

Over the next few months, my life appeared to be moving into another phase. I was feeling a need to use this newfound freedom to create a positive impact in other people's lives. I began to think about ways to help encourage people who had suffered trauma in their lives. I also began to wonder if there was a way to share some of the events of this hunting accident to help prevent others from becoming a victim of the same thing.

It was in the spring of 1980 that someone told me of the Virginia Game Department's Hunter Education program. Even after the accident, I never lost my love for the outdoors and for hunting, so this seemed like something I would enjoy being a part of. After a little research and a few phone calls, I was informed that the game department was looking for volunteer hunter education instructors and that they had a very comprehensive instructor training program. I was so excited at the possibility of turning a near tragedy into something that would possibly help save lives.

My first step was to take the hunter safety course, so I signed up for the next available class. After completing the course, the next step was to enroll in an instructor certification course. During the course, I shared my accident experience with some of the instructors who also served as game wardens from the Virginia Game

Department. One of the instructors, Dennis Mullins, was the investigating officer who had come to my home four years earlier to discuss the accident. I think he was pretty happy to see that I was trying to turn this event into something positive.

The instructor course was another step in the right direction for me, because every time I talked about the accident, it became easier. I was happy for the opportunity to talk to hunters, especially kids, about the importance of being safe with firearms and being sure of your target and beyond before discharging a firearm.

After the instructor certification, I had my first opportunity to teach a hunter education course. One of my challenges was to come up with a non-offensive way to talk about being shot to a child who wanted to be a hunter, without being too graphic or instilling fear. Even so, I wanted to implant in them the enormous responsibility they had when carrying a firearm into the woods or on a live firing range. The game department had created a great course for the experienced and non-experienced hunters and shooting sports enthusiasts. Using both video and text, they taught responsibility and accountability to hunters, and I was really proud to become a part of the program.

There is one particular side story, however, that I shall never forget. Every year, the game department would hold special advanced training courses at specified locations for a weekend. During that time I wanted all of the training I could receive, so each year I would attend the weekend training courses. As a result of the many specialty courses that they would offer, I achieved one of my personal goals, advancing to the level of Master Instructor.

It was during one of these weekend courses I discovered that the son of The Man who shot me years before had become a hunter education instructor himself. When he arrived at the weekend gathering, I immediately recognized the name and realized who he was. When he heard my name called at the roll call, it was obvious that he also knew who I was. That evening during the supper hour, I noticed that he was going out of his way to avoid me. I could tell he was very uncomfortable and that he felt awkward to be around me. In retrospect, I can understand how he felt.

The next morning, which was a Saturday, I decided I had to make a move to clear the air with this situation. I mean, this was a very nice guy, a born-again Christian, who was feeling awkward because his father had shot and nearly killed a guy who was sitting in the same room with him.

As he exited the dining hall after breakfast, I called his name. I walked over to him, extended my hand and said, "I know you are feeling uncomfortable about this whole situation, but no one here knows anything about it and as far as I am concerned, they will never know." I also told him that there were no hard feelings and suggested that we just relax and have a fun weekend. The expression on his face was priceless. It looked like a thousand pounds had just been lifted off his shoulders. He smiled and said "thank you," then shook my hand. God had blessed us both, using this incident to bring forth His goodness and power.

Even to this day, I am still active in the hunter education program. No one will ever know the number of lives that have been saved by that program. My love for the outdoors and my love for hunting has never waned. As a matter of fact, it has only increased as I have gotten older. Now, my passion for hunting and the outdoors is greater than ever, but my priorities are totally different. I love seeing wild game. I enjoy just watching deer or turkey, and the time of the harvest is kind of a sad time because it means that the hunt has ended.

Most of all, my time in the woods is a time that I feel a special closeness to God.

Chapter 13

SURVIVING THE TEEN YEARS

Over the next decade, my sons were growing into young men and my wife and I began to face the challenges of teenage sons. Like all parents, we were about to embark on a new chapter in our lives. I often secretly wondered if my worry and fear would return when my sons reached driving age. I wondered how much of that concern was a normal part of parenting and how much of it was a result of the PTSD.

When the boys eventually did get their driver's licenses, I was pretty nervous. After all, I remembered how I was as a teen driver. I won't be writing about that in this book! As a nervous father with a good memory, I decided to try a proactive approach to my sons and their driving habits. When it came time to get their license, I told them there were two main conditions. First, they could not have their license until they could pay the difference in the car insurance that would occur by adding them. Secondly, if anyone got a speeding ticket, I would take their license for one week for every mile per hour that they were cited for.

Rick did well, with no tickets until he was eighteen. Then the next year he got two in one trip to college in Florida. Tony didn't fare as well; he got his first ticket at the age of seventeen for driving fifty-two in a thirty-five-mph zone. Yes, I took his license. When we went to court and he testified to the judge that his dad had taken his license for seventeen weeks, the judge dropped the charges. My youngest son, Dan, never got a speeding ticket to my knowledge.

During their teen years especially, I was so thankful that I had learned to make God's Word a major part of my life. I really learned about placing them all in God's hands and trusting Him. Proverbs 3:5 says to "Trust in the Lord with all thine heart; and lean not unto thine own understanding" (KJV).

Yes, it's often easier said than done, but what a comfort to know we can trust in Him in the parts of our lives where we have no control. There were many times during these years that I had to begin to quote Scripture again. Of course I worried about my sons out on the highway, but I understood the weakness and know that God was faithful.

I will have to say that our family came through those teen years pretty well. Oh, there were some hard times, some extremely difficult times, and a few not-so-pleasant memories, but for the most part, they all made us very proud. However, I'm sure there were some events that Esther and I probably never want to hear about.

As years passed, I had all but forgotten about the hunting accident and it was just a shadow in my past. I could talk about it freely with no signs of emotion, and sometimes it almost seemed as if it had never even happened. It was during this time that I had to be reminded that in life, sometimes things are still going to be hard and trusting God is a choice and a lifestyle, not just a proclamation. As I experienced other trying times I found that there were many more promises that deal with fear and worry, not just 2 Timothy 1:7.

I also learned (and am still learning) that as long as we live, it is likely that we will experience traumatic events in our lives. There once was a time that I thought if I prayed for God's will or His blessing on a major decision in life such as a career decision or financial investment, and if I got a clear answer, then things should go smoothly with no problems. God has taught me that this is not the case.

Even when He gives us an answer to a specific request, it doesn't mean that there won't be disappointments or challenges. It is times such as this that we have to rely on God's Word to sustain us. Romans 8:28 tells us, "And we know that all things work together for good to those who love God, to those who are the called according to His purpose" (NKJV). This is not to say that we use God's Word like some sort of horoscope that we read for good luck and good fortune. It's simply taking His promises at face value and believing.

Another lesson I learned was that it is something that we have to practice daily. We have to study God's Word and apply it to our daily lives. His word is powerful and can be a major influence in our lives if we allow Him to speak to us through the Scriptures. As life has moved on, there have been many other times that I have found myself clinging to the hope and promise of His Word.

Chapter 14
A DREAM COME TRUE

The boys became men, finished college, got married, and began to bring other new lives into the family. I went on to maintain my career as a computer technician but as I got older, I found my passion for music and the guitar growing in a way that I had never experienced. I wanted to have a guitar in my hands every time there was a moment to spare.

Of course, by then Esther and I were grandparents and we were trying to help our aging parents as well, so spare time was at a minimum. Still, there were many nights that I would fall asleep downstairs on the sofa with a guitar in my hand.

I met some local guitarists and began to play some coffeehouse concerts around town. I had no idea that it was only whetting my appetite to begin a music ministry. Music was becoming a major part of my life again, and I began to feel that God was calling me to step out and minister with my guitar.

At an age when many musicians and artists were starting to cut back on touring and concerts, my true calling began to be realized and my ministry as a guitarist was born. I started playing my guitar at churches every weekend, and my testimony was a major part of every service. I started using my vacation time to travel farther. The ironic thing about it was that there were a few gospel singing groups and even a pastor who came to me to tell me that there was no way I could ever make it in gospel music or in ministry just playing guitar.

Nevertheless, I was getting invitations to speak at men's retreats, sportsman's dinners and even youth groups. By this time, I was nearing fifty years old and it felt as if my life was just taking off. Little did I know that my faith would soon be tested again. Everything I had been saying about faith for the past few years was about to be put to the test.

My music seemed to be gaining ground, and I had an increased hunger to step out in ministry. I started receiving invitations to play concerts and special events. Then Billy Hale, a friend of mine who owned a Christian radio station, asked me about recording a Christmas song for a compilation CD he was working on for radio release. In late fall of 1995, I went to a recording studio in Blountville, Tennessee, and recorded my first solo instrumental, "God Rest Ye Merry Gentlemen."

As a result of that recording, the next year I received my first award in gospel music. I was awarded the Bronze Cross Instrumentalist of the year with the International Country Gospel Music Association. That first awards show was in Zanesville, Ohio, and I was in total shock when they called my name. That great honor would be the first of more than eighty awards in our ministry.

I will never forget that drive to Zanesville. During our drive, Esther presented me with a gift. She unwrapped a box she had been hiding and opened it. The gift was a leather-bound date book. She started telling me she believed this date book would begin to fill with engagements all across the United States, where I would minister through music and testimony. She informed me that it was an expensive book that would last many years, and she was certain that our ministry would be lasting for years to come. Esther was visualizing us being in ministry full-time, and although it was my dream, I really never thought it could happen. My wife was always a visionary and a dreamer. I, on the other hand, was a realist. Even though I felt that my faith was strong, I always liked things in black and white.

Over the next few years it became evident that Esther was not only a visionary, she was a prayer warrior. The very next year, I was contacted by a friend who wanted to help sponsor my first CD. It was then that I began to record my first solo instrumental album. It was becoming evident that God had a plan for Esther and me in music ministry. As a statement of faith, we decided to name the project In His Hands.

Every night when I would go to the recording studio, Esther would spend time in prayer. It took about three months, but the recording was finally finished, mixed, mastered, and off to be duplicated. The day those boxes of one thousand CDs and five hundred cassette tapes arrived was a day of mixed emotions. On one hand, I was overwhelmed with excitement. On the other hand, I was thinking, how in the world will I ever get rid of all these

CDs and tapes? I tried to think of how many people I knew that might want to buy a cassette or CD. I felt a little sick; I thought I would never be able to sell them all.

I had no idea that this would be the first of many projects that would be heard all over the world. God was using my music and testimony to touch the hearts of people of all ages. My secret lifelong dream of being able to earn a living playing my guitar was slowly unfolding before my eyes.

In July of 1997, I attended the Chet Atkins Appreciation Society guitar convention in Nashville. I met so many great musicians and got to meet my hero, Chet Atkins, for the second time. I was like a kid in a candy store. For three and a half days, I walked around in awe of the excitement and the music, meeting some of the greatest guitarists in the world. I was living a dream.

During that first convention, I was traveling with a friend. I was unaware that he had signed my name on a list to perform during an open mike session on the main stage at the convention. I told him there was no way I could play in front of the guitarists that were there; he replied that I was already on the list to play, so I had to do it.

I don't think there was ever a time that I was as nervous as that day. My fifteen-minute set felt like an eternity. I was praying that my hands wouldn't tremble but would respond to what they had practiced for years.

I don't remember everything I played but I do remember that one of the songs was, "Amazing Grace." The only reason I remember that particular song is because after my set, there was a lady from the audience who met me in the lobby with tears in her eyes. She shared with me that the song had touched her heart. I was so relieved to know that even in my state of nervousness, the music would still touch someone's heart. I felt so honored that God would use me even at a venue such as this to minister.

Chapter 15

A NEW BATTLE

When I returned home from Nashville, I was still on an emotional high. Of course, it didn't take long to return to the real world of daily routine and trying to earn a living. Two weeks after my return I was sent to Atlanta, Georgia, for a week-long class at our national training center.

That Wednesday night, I was out taking a walk and began to experience something that would again change my life. As I was walking I began to feel a tightness and pain in my chest. When I stopped to rest, the pain would subside. When I started walking again, it would return.

The next night, I called Esther at home and told her that I would need to see a doctor as soon as I got home on Friday. When I got home I went to see my doctor that same afternoon. She did an EKG which showed normal results, but there was still something there that gave her cause for concern. She said she was going to make an appointment for me to have a stress test the next week.

As I was standing out at the receptionist's desk about to leave, the doctor walked out and asked if I would consider going to see a cardiologist right away. She had already called him, and he was waiting for me. When I saw the cardiologist and described my symptoms, he told me that a stress test was not necessary because he strongly suspected that I had some blockage in my heart.

He scheduled a cardiac catheterization for the following Tuesday morning. In the short time it took me to drive home, the realization that I could actually have a heart problem was filling my mind with anxiety once again. After twenty-five years of being free from the prison of fear, I became aware that my dependence on God's promises needed to become a lifestyle and not just a past experience.

As I was going through the hospital admissions procedures that next Tuesday, I inwardly chuckled, thinking that even if a person had no problems with fear, checking into a hospital for that kind of procedure would scare anyone to death. They tell you that with a heart catheterization, you have a one in one thousand chance of dying. Even though those odds are very much in your favor, it still causes you to think when they ask you to sign that paper declaring that you have been informed.

After the procedure, I was informed that I did have two blockages and needed to have bypass surgery immediately. They scheduled it for the very next day. I thought I was really being brave and taking everything in stride, but I began to worry that night when I went to bed. Sometimes the mind can be our worst enemy, and this night was one of those cases.

As I lay there, I started to think about the things that could happen, all the "what ifs". What if the doctor made just a 1mm mistake? What if my heart would not start after the surgery? What if I did not wake up from the anesthesia? My wife was lying beside me there in bed, but

I still felt so alone and afraid.

Esther was still awake, so I asked her to pray. She laid her hand over on my chest and began to pray for me. All of a sudden, as I recalled my favorite Scripture passage, God swept a peace over me that was unmistakable. Within a few minutes, I was sleeping soundly.

The bypass procedure went without incident, and within four days, I was at home recuperating. It's at such times that we begin to realize there is a difference between being a little nervous or even scared about facing a major event like surgery, and being obsessed with fear. We all have a natural fear of the unknown; that's normal. We all have some fear of things that are totally out of our control. That, too, is normal. The problem seems to be when that fear begins to overshadow our ability to function and to reason.

I think we all experience fear over certain areas of our lives. Some just seem to be better at hiding it than others. Maybe it could be better stated that there is a difference in natural fear and what the Bible calls "the spirit of fear." That "spirit" is definitely not of God. The Word of God is a great weapon to battle fear. It's like having a fire extinguisher in your home—not because you worry about it catching fire, but because it is a tool that might help you overcome a fire, should it occur. God's Word can be just that tool for your spiritual house.

Serious health conditions and other difficult trials that we encounter are not easy to go through, but they can impart a blessing—they teach us how special every day of our life is, and that each day is a gift from God to live as if it could be our last. Every day we experience is an investment in eternity.

One thing I learned about open-heart surgery is that sometimes major surgery of this magnitude can often generate its own kind of Post-Traumatic Stress Disorder. I have never heard doctors call it that, but my surgeon did warn me that there is a possibility of high emotions and depression for up to a year after surgery.

I don't know if we are just made more aware of our own mortality or the actual procedure causes it, but I do know the depression and emotionalism was very real. There were times I would start to cry for no reason at the most inopportune times, such as a family get-together or a special function. It seldom would occur when I was alone but seemed to hit when I was in public. I would often joke during those times that I could cry at a cartoon.

I began to realize that I was going to be dealing with some of the symptoms of PTSD for the rest of my life. Coming to this realization was a milestone for me. I knew that because of my relationship with Christ, I was not in this battle alone and that I could prevail. Matthew 28:20 says

"Teaching them to observe all things whatsoever I have commanded you: and, lo, I am with you always, even unto the end of the world. Amen" (NKJV).

About a year after my heart surgery, I was invited to fly

up to New Hampshire for several days of concerts. It was the first time I had ventured out alone since the surgery. After the second day I suddenly started to feel sick, and all I wanted to do was sleep and lie around. I had no appetite and felt like I was losing strength day by day. I didn't want to think I was homesick, but that's exactly what was happening. I was suffering from separation anxiety so severely that it was making me physically ill.

My doctor explained to me later that I had developed a sense of security by being close to the hospital and my cardiologist, not to mention my wife, upon whom I had been so dependent for the past year. I couldn't understand any of this because during my career as a technician, I traveled alone all the time, often for weeks at a time. That time, as so many others, I had to be reminded that in Christ, we are never alone and sometimes we have to depend on the Great Comforter to give us the strength to face uncertainty. By His strength, I did finish the week-long concert tour.

Chapter 16

SAYING GOODBYE

I found myself being invited to play full concerts in churches around the country. It seems funny now, but for the first few church concerts I played, I would try to go with someone else who could be part of the concert because I was not convinced that my guitar playing would minister effectively to people. I was not sure if there was anything I could say that could touch people's hearts or lives.

After only a few concerts, however, my music list began to grow. I began to realize that I had much to say. I found myself telling the story of the hunting accident and sharing how God had touched my life and delivered me from PTSD through that Scripture in 2 Timothy. Every service and every concert would bring a new experience, and the responses were overwhelming. I would get cornered after the services by Vietnam veterans who were still going through PTSD. I would also be stopped by moms and even teenagers who were experiencing bouts with fear and anxiety. I was honored, yet humbled to have an opportunity to be used of God in such an awesome way.

One special night I played a concert in another state. I was staying with some friends and after the concert, they invited another couple over for some refreshments. While the hosts were preparing the food, I stepped out into the garage to get my guitar out of the car. The other guest was standing out in the open garage, smoking a cigarette.

When I approached the car he walked by me and went to shut the door to the inside, shutting me in the garage. He then walked right up to me with a strange look on his face. I have to admit, it was a little intimidating. He raised up his hand and began to point his finger at me and by now, I was really shook.

He then said, with trembling lips, "I need to know if that Scripture will work for me. I'm a Vietnam veteran and everything you said in your testimony tonight about fear, you spoke directly to me. I have tried everything from drugs to alcohol, and nothing has worked. I have to have some help!"

I responded, "Yes, I truly believe it will help you. Let's pray." Right there in the garage, I placed my hand on his shoulder and we prayed. He shared with me over a year later about how much that Scripture had changed his life.

As God continued to bless the ministry, my world was soon to be shaken again. During the next two years, my parents' health began to fail. Dad was in and out of the hospital with congestive heart failure. His first heart attack was in 1996. I remember vividly the doctor coming out into the hall to tell us that Dad's heart was only functioning at about twenty percent and he likely wouldn't survive the night. Needless to say I was pretty devastated, but I was also concerned about the spiritual state of my dad's heart.

When I went into the room that night to see him, my pastor, Joe Burnside, was with me. Dad was on a breathing machine and so weak he could barely open his eyes, but that night, with a very weak squeezing of his hand to respond, Dad accepted Christ as his Lord and Savior. Many tears of joy were shed that night. The awesome part was that three weeks later, he was dismissed from the hospital and God gave him three more years of life. When my father passed in 1999, I was reminded that we can't always understand God's plans but we must still trust Him.

Aside from trying to minister on the road and maintain a full-time job, I would go by my parents' house several times a week to check up on them, do work around the house, or run errands. Mom began to experience ministrokes and would often fall. Dad just seemed to be getting weaker by the month.

Then in February 1999, Mom fell and apparently hit her head on the dresser. She was hospitalized and after emergency surgery, she went into a coma. The next four weeks turned out to be the longest four weeks of my life. Dad suffered another heart attack and was in the Cardio Intensive Care Unit of the hospital while Mom was in the Neuro Intensive Care Unit.

The hospital was very good about letting me stay there most of the time. The only time I went home was to shower and change. The nurses even showed me how to set up oxygen bottles and regulators for Dad, so I could take him in a wheelchair to visit Mom. It was heartbreaking to watch him hold her hand and talk to her, knowing she could not hear him.

Four weeks after her fall, Mom passed away. The night of her death, Dad was in a mood to tell stories about them in their younger years. He shared things I never knew about them. Even though Dad was not an outwardly sentimental type of person, I think I really understood then how much he loved her over their fifty-plus years of marriage. That's a gift I will treasure for life.

Two days later, the day of Mom's funeral, I went by to visit Dad. I said how it saddened me that he would not be able to attend the funeral. He simply said he would rather go be with her. That afternoon at 1:00 p.m., Mom's funeral began with me playing "It Is Well with My Soul." At 1:05 p.m., Dad went on to be with the Lord.

I can't explain the pain and grief of losing both parents three days apart, but looking back, God knew best. There were so many special stories about Mom and Dad that transpired during that time, but one special story needs to be told. We discovered just a week before Mom's passing that she had accidentally let their life insurance policies lapse. When Esther discovered this and came and told me, I replied, "I just don't believe God is going to leave this on us."

The total cost of both funerals was more than ten thousand dollars. I had no idea of this but at the time of their passing, there was a Christian radio station near Cabot, Arkansas, that had been playing my music quite a lot over the past year. The program director had even held a special tribute to my ministry that Saturday.

A month later when I resumed my concert schedule, I flew to Arkansas. After three nights of concerts, the friends I was staying with called me to their living room the last night I was there. My friend, Larry, reminded me that the Christian radio station in Cabot had been playing my music for over a year. When they heard about the death of my parents, they held a special hour-long radio broadcast to talk about my music and ministry, and they featured my CDs. They made a copy of the radio show and gave it to Larry for me.

The night before I was scheduled to leave, Larry presented me with the tape of the radio show and a basket full of cards and letters from friends and fans from all over the state. There was also nearly $2,000 in cash and checks. Within three months, the entire funeral expense was paid and not one dollar came out of our pocket. God is good all the time.

Chapter 17

STRETCHING MY WINGS

Less than a year after my mom and dad passed away, in late fall of 2000, I received an invitation to fly to Sweden to share my music. Needless to say, I was very nervous about this. I mean, we were talking about flying six thousand miles away to a different country and a different culture. How was I to know they would even accept my music?

After talking my youngest son, Dan, into going with me, I eventually agreed to make a two-week tour. With the help of Lars Svenson, a friend from Sweden, I found myself booked in seven churches, two music conservatories, and a music store.

We arrived in Sweden, and after a day of resting and trying to overcome the jet lag, we were settling in. The weather those first few days was damp and cold, and the days were shorter because of the latitude. But we were staying with the Svenson family, and they were wonderful hosts.

As it was my first time to visit this beautiful country, I observed a number of interesting things about the culture—especially the delicious food! Every church served coffee and some sort of cheese, crackers, and pastries after every service.

After one service, they served a meal that was unlike anything I'd had before. I can't remember what it was called, but it was in the form of a large cake. Every slice contained salad, an entree which was some sort of chicken or beef, bread, and even dessert.

The Swedish cheeses were wonderful, and their coffee was always strong. Lars told me Americans didn't know how to enjoy coffee because we always brewed it much too weak.

Dan and I also enjoyed a little pizza shop we found in the small town where we were living. They served a pizza that was called a kebab. It was a pie with shredded beef and a white cream sauce over it, smothered in cheese. We went there just about every day for lunch. When we walked to the pizza shop, we passed by this small gas station that sold fresh Swedish pastries. Those pastries were probably the best I ever tasted.

The church services were a bit different than churches in the United States, but everyone was very warm and friendly. One of the places I was invited to play was a music conservatory in a city called Jonkoping. I think it was pronounced "yonshipping." I am not a trained musician, and I was about to play for a group of highly educated musicians. Instead of trying to impress this group with fast chops and guitar riffs, I felt that it was a time to ask God for a special anointing. I didn't talk to them about music; I shared with them about how special it was to be called into a ministry where I could share my passion for music.

After the presentation, one of the students came

to me and shared how he was encouraged. He was an experienced musician who wanted to share the gospel through his music but his parents wanted him to play in a Swedish rock band where he could make lots of money. All he wanted was a little encouragement that following God's calling was the right thing to do. That day, God was using me not to impress or entertain, but to encourage one of His own who felt a calling on his life. This young man was fighting the fear of criticism and ridicule from his family. Here was another manifestation of that "spirit of fear." The irony was that I had battled that same "spirit of fear" in making this trip. After all, I was in a different country with a different culture and a language barrier.

At one church I was asked to play at a luncheon for a group of Swedish senior citizens. Since I could not speak the language, I was aided by an interpreter. I shared some Scripture and testimony through the interpreter, but mostly I just played my guitar.

After the luncheon, the interpreter and I started talking. We were near a table where six older men were sitting drinking coffee and obviously having a discussion. Of course, I had no idea what they were saying, but the interpreter began to lean his ear in their direction. He said, "Oh my, they are talking about you." I responded, "Really?" Again he said, "Oh my."

With a bit of impatience in my voice, I said, "What? What are they saying"? His response brought me to tears, and it very likely changed my outlook on this ministry forever. He told me that one of the men said to the others.

"As the music man was up there playing, it was almost as if the hand of God was there playing music just for us." I walked away in tears, realizing that God had used me in a special way. I felt so unworthy that He allowed me to be used in that way.

At another service, there was a very distinguished gentleman dressed in a black hat and black topcoat. He came back and greeted us after the concert and told me he enjoyed the music and that I would hear from him very soon. I honestly didn't think any more about it, but two days later he called Lars' home and asked to speak to me.

He told me that he wanted Dan and me to stop over in Stockholm before we left to fly back to the States, and he wanted to take us on a personal tour through the old city of Stockholm. We both were excited about this even though we had no idea who the gentleman was. It turned out, he was the Scandinavian division chief editor for Reader's Digest, and also a seven-time world champion of Jeopardy.

Since we were not scheduled to fly out of Stockholm, I called the airlines and changed our return flight and we got on the X2000 fast train for a 200-mile trip to Stockholm. This train travels the beautiful countryside at 125 mph. In turns, the tracks are banked, making the ride so quiet and smooth that we could drink coffee with no risk of spilling it.

The next morning we met the gentleman, whose name

was Mr. Andersen, at the hotel in Stockholm. In his black wool topcoat and hat and his proud distinguished look, he reminded me of Alfred Hitchcock.

There is a funny story that happened with Mr. Andersen. The old city of Stockholm is made up of many small islands, and he took us all through its narrow streets and small bridges. He was like a walking encyclopedia of interesting history and facts as we visited places that few Americans had ever seen. We visited cathedrals with sculptures that were breathtaking.

As we walked on the centuries-old stone streets, I was reminded of how young our nation of America actually is. Mr. Andersen told us the stories behind historic statues with great pride in his heritage. During our tour, I sincerely thanked him for his kindness in sharing his time with us. As a way to show our appreciation, I told him I would be honored to treat him to lunch. He politely nodded and kept walking and telling stories.

After a couple of hours we came to a beautiful building that he said was the Royal Opera House. Next to the entrance of the opera house there was a quaint restaurant, where Mr. Andersen proudly stated that kings and emperors attended and dined daily. Then he said, "We shall dine here?" I turned to Dan with a look that said, "Me and my big mouth—how am I going to pay for this?"

We walked inside and a waiter dressed in a suit walked over to greet Mr. Andersen. Even though I could not understand what they were saying, it was evident he was a regular customer there. As they led us to a beautiful table with four plush, leather-bound chairs, I was about to lose my appetite wondering how I was going to pay for this without showing any sign of concern.

The meal was wonderful and when the check came, the amount was in Swedish krona, so I had no idea what it was. I handed him my Visa card and secretly prayed, God, let this card go through without being declined. Thankfully, the card was approved and the bill turned out to be around seventy-five dollars in American money. I'm sure the bill was more than that, knowing the kind of establishment it was, but another lesson learned. Still, it was a great way to end a wonderful eleven-day ministry tour.

As we boarded the plane out of Stockholm, I reflected on the trip and thanked God for blessing us in so many ways. I realized that even though there was a language barrier, sometimes God speaks through instrumental music even more powerfully than through spoken words. As it says in 1 Samuel 16:23, "Whenever the spirit from God came on Saul, David would take up his lyre and play. Then relief would come to Saul; he would feel better, and the evil spirit would leave him" (NIV).

Chapter 18

STEP OF FAITH

The next year would prove to be the turning point of my musical career. I turned fifty-five years old and had worked as a service tech for thirty-three years. At age fifty-five and a half, I would be able to take early retirement with full benefits. It seemed that I was busy enough with the music ministry to make it, but an attack of the "what ifs" began to slow my ability to make a decision. After all, I had a fairly secure job, the pay was okay, and the benefits were good. It was a good security blanket, because I had accrued enough vacation time to make long weekends and stay busy.

Every time I would be about ready to make a commitment and step out in faith, believing God would meet our needs, fear would strike again. What if I couldn't get enough dates? What if I got sick? What if, what if.... Then, a pastor friend gave me this reminder: If God calls, He will provide. As it says in Proverbs 3:5–6, "Trust in the Lord with all thine heart and lean not unto thine own understanding. In all thy ways acknowledge him and he shall direct thy paths" (KJV).

I came to the realization that it was time to dive in and swim. Sometimes we ask for God's guidance, when what we are really asking for is the promise that our life will be free of worry. After all, if it's God's will, what could go wrong? The fact is, that is not the real world. We are still going to experience pain, suffering and problems. Cars are still going to break down at the most inopportune time. Our kids are still going to get sick, and bills will still be in the mailbox.

It was in late September of 2001 that Esther and I decided it was time for me to retire from my job and commit to full-time ministry. We decided that Esther would continue to work for at least one more year, which would serve as our emergency parachute. It sounded like a good idea to me at the time; however, I was miserable that first year traveling alone. After about ten months, we decided that if "we" were going to be in full-time ministry, then it meant both of us and not just me. It turned out to be one of the best decisions we ever made. God wanted this ministry endeavor to be Richard and Esther, not just Richard.

That first year as a team started off great. We had three months booked in Florida, I had just received an endorsement with McPherson guitars, and life was good. I was playing in RV resorts all over the state and two or three churches every weekend.

Then one Tuesday morning, after we'd been in Florida for around a month, I was phoning the pastors whose churches I was booked in the following Sunday. When I dialed the first church, the secretary answered. I introduced myself, told her that I was scheduled for a concert there on Sunday morning, and asked to speak with the pastor to discuss plans for the service.

After briefly putting me on hold, the secretary came back on the line and said the pastor was busy and couldn't talk. She then passed along a message from him—he was sorry, but he had something else planned for Sunday. I politely told her this had been scheduled since November and I had sent all the promo material over a month ago. She said she was sorry and that if the pastor changed his mind, he would call. Then, with a "click," the line went dead.

The hurt and frustration I experienced at that moment was overwhelming. I told Esther I needed to go for a walk, and I stepped out of the motorhome. There was a small lake behind the coach and I took a walk down to the lake, sat down on a rock, and began to pray. I'm not sure it was even a prayer. I was crying, and I looked up to the sky and said out loud, "God, have You laid me off already? I mean, I quit my job to come down here and do this, and You allow this to happen to me? What is going on?"

I then said, "I need to hear from you before this day is over; I need to know if this ministry means anything to you." It was a bold prayer, but I was pretty desperate.

As I went through the day, I did not forget the prayer. I was expecting God to give me a great revelation or epiphany, but nothing was happening, and I was pretty discouraged. Through the night as I was watching TV, I kept watching the clock and thinking, God, you are running out of time. Still nothing. Around 10:00 p.m., as she always does, Esther went to bed. She knew I was pretty depressed but other than silently praying, she had no idea what to do.

That night at about 11:30, as I was checking my email, I saw a message from a name I didn't recognize. It read something like this: "Dear Richard, you don't know me but I was in one of your outdoor concerts three years ago. I had just discovered that my wife was having an affair and my world as I knew it was over. I had not slept for a week. After your concert, I purchased a couple of your CDs, and when I went to bed that night I went to sleep listening to your music. It touched my heart and gave me such peace, I could finally sleep. The next morning was a Sunday morning. I found myself in church and accepted Christ as my Savior. I just wrote to thank you for being there for me and because of your music, we are brothers in Christ. May God bless you and your ministry."

Needless to say, I was crying so hard I could no longer even see the computer screen. I was so emotional, I took the laptop to the bedroom. I literally dropped it on the bed and woke Esther up. At first she was startled and wanted to know what was wrong. Then, she picked up the laptop and began to read. We both shared a time of tears and rejoicing, knowing that God had heard my prayer. The time was 11:55 p.m. After that night, I never again questioned my calling.

The rest of 2002 was looking much more positive. My schedule and my little leather date book were filling up fast with concert dates as well as more contacts. It seemed as if my life was on track and everything was looking up. I had just recorded my fourth CD, and the first album, In His Hands, was in its third pressing. I had received a number of gospel music awards, including Instrumentalist of the Decade from the International Country Gospel Music Association. We were seeing souls won to Christ. Life was good.

In April of that year, however, we were again made aware that life can be unpredictable, that we never know what tomorrow holds. I was in Dallas, Texas, visiting a friend after finishing a series of concerts in Abilene. Three days before I was scheduled to return home, I received a phone call at about 2:00 a.m. The call was to notify me that my oldest son, Rick, and his wife, Kelly, were on the way to the hospital. Kelly was eight months pregnant, and the baby's heart had stopped beating. She was going to have to deliver her first son, Brandon Richard, knowing that he had no heartbeat.

The plane ride from Dallas was without a doubt the longest trip I had ever experienced. I arrived late that morning and that evening, Kelly delivered her lifeless son. I thought I had experienced pain before, but never like this. It was twofold. I had lost a newborn grandson, but watching my son and his wife go through the grief of losing their firstborn was unbearable. After all, I am a dad; I am supposed to be able to fix things and take care of my sons, no matter how old they are. That's what dads do. I don't think I have ever felt so helpless.

There was a beautiful memorial service for little baby Brandon. Little did we know that even in his passing, he would leave a legacy. Rick and Kelly have been able to minister to other parents who have lost children, and Rick wrote a novel about losing a son titled Forever My Son.

God also gave Rick and Kelly two beautiful daughters, Katelyn and Lauren. And, Rick is now the author of five children's books. Through that heart-wrenching experience, God showed us that even through tragedy and pain, He can bring something good out of it that will enrich the lives of others.

Chapter 19

TIMING IS EVERYTHING

Another of the great things about being a Christian is how God seems to choreograph events in our lives, in His timing, causing things to happen that we could never plan in a million years. Take, for example, the day I met a man named Roger Rankin at the annual Chet Atkins Appreciation Society convention in Nashville. He came to my product table, introduced himself, and said he would like to bring me to his little hometown in southeast Kansas. What I didn't know was that Roger would help to change the scope of my ministry forever.

That first year, all I did was give him a business card, and he left. Three years passed, and he returned to my table at the very same event—only he was different. He had an ascot around his neck and was a few pounds lighter. He told me how he had battled throat cancer as a result of smoking and tobacco use. He had to talk through a buzzer pressed against his throat. Even with no vocal cords, Roger could communicate very well and as I learned over the next few years, his sense of humor was relentless.

At that second meeting, Roger again asked when I was coming to his hometown. I told him if he would book me there for a week, I would come.

Weeks later, he called me on the phone. He spoke with the buzzer in a monotone, speaking very slowly and repeating a lot of his words. He told me he had some concerts set up in his town of Longton, Kansas, and we agreed on a date. He warned me that it was a small town, but he assured me that they would love my music.

That first year, he had me scheduled to play at the local high school and the town hall. I think the town population was about 374, and the hall was packed. We parked our motorhome at Roger's farm, which is where I learned just what a jokester he was and what a great sense of humor he had.

We returned the next year and parked at the farm again. Roger had a cow with a newborn calf, and one evening, he decided to pen the calf up right behind our motorhome but keep the mother cow out in the pasture. Needless to say, Esther and I didn't sleep much that night! The next morning, bright and early, Roger came knocking on our door, laughing through his buzzer and asking how we slept. He took us to the town café that morning for breakfast just so he could tell everyone the story and share a laugh.

Another time when we arrived, he informed me that he had entered us in a bass-fishing tournament as a team. It was a fundraiser for one of the local churches, and the money would go to support a mission trip. Roger informed me that at this tournament, everyone would check in that morning and split up as teams to fish. I asked where we would be fishing and whose boat we would use. He laughed and told me that everyone would fish in the farm pond of their choice, with no boats needed. We were to weigh our catches in at 3:00 p.m., then clean all the fish and have a community fish fry. Now that's my kind of fishing! When we left for our pond that he had already chosen, I started bragging and joking with him about how badly I was going to embarrass him by catching all the fish.

I was using a jerk bait called "Fin-S Fish." The lake was about a foot or so low, which meant I had to walk out into the mud to cast my line. It started working for me and after a few casts, I was reeling in a two-pound-plus largemouth. I showed it to Roger and laughed and asked for a stringer. His buzzer was in his pocket so he just clicked his mouth twice and pointed to the truck.

I went to the truck and found the stringer. It was an old one with safety-pin style clips on a rope. I clipped the bass on the first one, went to the edge of the water as close as I could get, and tossed the fish into the water. After about thirty minutes I had my limit of fish and started culling them, exchanging smaller catches for larger ones.

I was really busting Roger up over this, making fun of him because he had only caught a couple of fish. The next fish I caught was the largest so far and I was ready to quit, knowing I had the winning stringer. After adding that fish, I showed the stringer to Roger, boasting all the while.

I approached the water's edge with a heave, tossed my bounty back into the water to keep them alive. Well, as Roger watched, when I released the stringer, the end broke and every single fish slid off the rope with the clips in their mouths. They were jumping in the shallow water, and some were tail-dancing as if to say, "See ya!" Roger was sitting on the bank, laughing so hard he was almost choking. It goes without saying that we did not win the tourney, but that year for Christmas, Roger sent me a gift-wrapped, all-metal fishing stringer.

Roger knew my love for hunting and fishing. One time, he came into the driveway after an errand and told me there was a camera crew from the Outdoor Channel with a guy named Ivan Hawthorne. Ivan was the owner and founder of C'Mere Deer, a company that sells products to attract deer. They were filming a Kansas whitetail deer hunt there nearby, and Roger told me I should go to the café and meet Ivan. We jumped into the truck, and to the café we went. I walked in, introduced myself to Ivan, and talked with him for a few minutes. I never dreamed that this encounter would begin a new friendship that would open more doors in our ministry.

There were many stories that could be shared about Roger. He was a good guitar player and a funny guy, but most of all he was a special friend who made me a better person. He fought a hard and painful battle with cancer, but he never lost his joy, his faith, or his love for God and people. He went to the schools with me and would tell kids what tobacco could do to the body. He was an ambassador for my ministry, our Lord, and anything he believed in. When he passed away a few years ago, it was quite a loss for everyone who knew him.

The spring after I met Ivan Hawthorne, I received a phone call from one of his friends, who asked if I would be interested in participating in a spring turkey hunt with Kids Hunting for a Cure. Through various outdoor events for adults and kids, this nonprofit organization raises funds for St. Jude's and other hospitals and foundations dedicated to developing cures for cancer and childhood diseases.

Excited to work with Kids Hunting for a Cure, I adjusted my schedule so I could be there the weekend of the hunt. On Friday night there was a big expo with food, celebrities from the Outdoor Channel, a turkey calling contest, and a concert where I played and shared my testimony about the hunting accident.

The next morning I went hunting with a twelve-year-old boy who had never hunted, and who had recently lost his dad to cancer. I was able to call in two gobblers and video the boy harvesting his first turkey. We were the first team to report in to the center with a harvest, and the young man was smiling from ear to ear. A few years later, he wrote me a letter to thank me for sharing that time with him and ministering to him, and to let me know he was living for Christ. Events like these keep us aware that the mission field is not inside the church walls.

Chapter 20

HIS MYSTERIOUS WAYS

I must confess that along my ministry journey, there have been times I have found myself far out of my comfort zone. In such situations, I have even wondered, Why am I here? I don't want to be here.

I have also discovered that God has neither time nor distance barriers. We tend to rationalize that if we travel hundreds of miles, it must be for a group or a greater plan. Yet God may send us halfway across the country to touch the life of one individual if we are open to His will. He has often surprised me, using me in ways I didn't expect and even in places I didn't expect.

On one such occasion, I was invited to travel about 700 miles to play at a benefit concert for a three-year-old girl with cancer, so I agreed to go. The event was supposed to take place from noon until night and feature two gospel groups, two country music groups, and two rock groups. When I arrived, I discovered that this was definitely not the case. There were no other gospel groups. There was one country band and a bunch of rock groups. There were also beer kegs and lots of drinking and partying. To be honest, I was going to leave; I felt so out of place. I called Esther, explained the situation, and asked her to pray because I had no idea what to do. She promised to be praying at the time I was to go on stage.

There were hundreds of people there and as the day

progressed, things were getting wilder and many were drinking and dancing in front of the stage. By then, I was thinking I would surely be booed and laughed off the stage when I started playing solo instrumentals, especially gospel music. The two mainstream bands had pretty good lead guitarists who were obviously convinced of just how good they were. They were giving quite a show. The rock player was dressed in skin-tight jeans and a vest with no shirt, and he had lots of piercings and long hair—quite a contrast from what would follow.

Just before I was scheduled to go on, the parents of the little girl asked me to come to their trailer. It was a sanitized, germ-free environment for the child. I went in to visit her and could tell that she was afraid. After all, she equated strangers with needles and pain. Her parents thanked me for being a part of this and I asked if I could pray for the girl. We held hands and I said a prayer.

It was then that I began to have a peace about why I was there. At the time that I was to walk on stage, they brought the child up to be introduced. I picked up a microphone and said with a loud voice, "This is why we are here and there is only one person we can turn to at a time like this—God." The entire pavilion got totally silent. As I started to play I could see people putting their drinks down, walking back into the pavilion, and finding seats. The other two lead guitarists ran up the aisle and literally slid into their seats on the front row. It was like they were entranced by everything I played and said.

After I did my set, I was walking back to my motorhome

somewhat relieved that it was over, but rejoicing because I knew God's presence was there. I don't remember now what I played or said, but I knew He had used me on that stage. All of a sudden, both guitar players came up to me and began to talk as they followed me to the motorhome. They told me how blown away they were by my music, and they asked if they could come inside. They began to ask questions about the music and certain riffs that I played on stage, but soon the conversation started turning toward religion and why I was doing what I was doing.

The country player told me about a health issue his daughter had, and he asked if I would be willing to pray for his child and his marriage. Just then, there was a knock at the door. It was his wife, with a cup of beer in her hand. He invited her in, but told her not to bring the beer in, since we were about to pray for their baby girl. The other guitarist also asked if I could pray with him. We were all crying tears of joy, and I suddenly realized that this was all part of God's plan in bringing me there. He can use us even when we are out of our comfort zone. In fact, sometimes I think that is where we can be most effective.

During the next several years my concert schedule continued to become busier. We began traveling in a diesel motorhome, averaging 180 to 200 days on the road some years, but we both were loving every minute of it. I was playing in all sorts of venues, from dinner theaters to RV resorts to sportsmen's banquets to festivals and, always, churches. We also started getting more invitations to schools.

On one trip out west, we were in eastern Missouri. After a church concert I was invited to go to a friend's house to play in a jam session. While I was there I met a man named Donnie Quick, who said he had a special guitar he wanted me to try. He went out to his car and came back with a black guitar gig bag. I noticed he was acting like it was a bit heavy, and when he opened the case, I immediately saw why. There was a stainless steel muffler with twin tailpipes attached and a neck from a guitar. It was a guitar!

I couldn't believe this guy had built a guitar out of a 1968 Thunderbird muffler. I picked it up and it was very heavy and awkward to hold and play, but very cool. It was all chrome plated and had a seat belt made into a strap, and it sounded pretty good. As I strummed this unusual guitar, my mind was racing, thinking of places where it would be effective. After I played a few tunes on it, Donnie suggested I take it on the road with me for about a year. Of course I jumped at the chance. Soon it became a regular part of my concerts, especially men's functions and events held at schools.

A pastor friend of mine suggested that I come up with a way to make the muffler guitar smoke while I played it. I thought that was a great idea, so we began to brainstorm. He suggested a stage fog machine, so we purchased one at a music store. The next trick was to get the fog to the guitar. After a lot of experimenting, I came up with the idea to splice a vacuum hose and oxygen hose running into the inlet pipe of the muffler. It worked great! People really enjoyed seeing this "smokin'" guitar in action.

After about a year of touring with the muffler guitar, I received a call from Donnie. He informed me that he was going to need the guitar back, because he had received an invitation to display all of his different muffler guitars at the Missouri State Fair. He said he needed it as soon as possible, so I told him I would ship it back right away.

After I hung up the phone, I immediately went into panic mode. This guitar had been such a great tool over the past year, and the kids were loving it everywhere I went. I said a prayer and decided to call him back. I told him what an important tool the muffler guitar was and asked if there was any way I could purchase it from him. When he discovered how I was using it in schools and for special men's functions, he readily agreed and gave me an unbelievably good price. Needless to say, I sent him a check right away. Over the years, this crazy muffler guitar has become a "brand" of this ministry—just one more example of God's plan.

As Esther and I traveled across the country, God continued to move in even more unexpected ways. Through a friend in Ohio, I was introduced to a very colorful and spirited Floridian named Eileen, who would become a lifelong friend. When we met she was in her early seventies, but I don't think I have ever met a more energetic lady.

Eileen was the events coordinator for the National

Hot Rod Association. She quickly discovered that I was a big fan of the NHRA and drag racing. In my younger years I had attended many drag racing events all around Virginia. I knew the names of all the drivers and the class of dragsters that they drove. Never in my wildest dreams did I imagine that years later through my music ministry, I would have the opportunity to meet so many of these drivers.

Eileen asked me if I would be interested in going with her to the NHRA Hall of Fame banquet that year, where I would be sitting with drag racing legends like Don Garlits, Ronnie Sox, and many other superstars. I also discovered that Eileen herself was, in fact, a member of the NHRA Hall of Fame.

At that banquet, I was introduced to the chaplain of an organization called "Racers for Christ." When Eileen told him about my music ministry and especially about the muffler guitar, he invited me to come to the Gatornationals drag racing event in Gainesville, Florida, to play and speak for the chapel service on Sunday morning. Of course, I accepted the invitation.

At the event, I shared my testimony in front of hundreds of racecar drivers and their crew members, telling them how God had healed me from nightmares and panic attacks. Not surprisingly, the muffler guitar was a big hit. The greatest part of the service, however, was that when we extended an invitation for prayer, there were seven race car drivers and crew members who came forward and accepted Christ as their Savior. What an awesome thrill that was!

The icing on the cake was that I got to spend two days at the Gatornationals and had an all-access pass to the pit area with all the drivers and crew. A few of the drivers even invited me into their restricted crew areas. To this day, I still get to go to the Nationals and work with Racers for Christ.

Chapter 21

FAITH IN THE MIDST
OF THE STORM

Everything was going great for us for a while. Esther and I were living the dream, so to speak. We were busy traveling all across the country and God was blessing. Then, life happened again.

During November of 2006, I began to experience chest pains. After a visit to my cardiologist and another heart catheterization, he discovered I had another blocked artery and would need a stent. The procedure went fine, and I was sent home for a few weeks with restrictions which kept me off the road for a month.

In January, I resumed my tour and things appeared to be back to normal. But then, about six weeks after the procedure, I was doing some concerts in Florida and began to have chest pains once again. A close friend drove Esther and me to the emergency room in Sarasota. They did an emergency heart catheterization and discovered that the stent that was installed in November was a non-drug-eluting stent and that it had blocked.

I was awake during the catheterization procedure and the cardiologist explained to me that it was very dangerous to reinstall a new stent inside the old stent after it was unblocked. He introduced me to the anesthesiologist and informed me that if there was a problem, they would be prepping me for emergency open heart surgery.

I felt scared and all alone, and Esther was in the waiting room, not knowing what is happening. A pastor friend was sitting with her giving her comfort, and I was thinking I might not wake up and could soon be facing eternity. One minute life was good—we were traveling and making music—and the next minute I found myself in the catheterization lab, wondering if I would even get to see my wife again. I closed my eyes and whispered a prayer for God's comfort and protection.

Even in the midst of this frightening situation, Esther and I were reminded of God's faithfulness and His perfect timing. An hour or so after I prayed that prayer, I was lying in the recovery room and the nurse asked me how I managed to get connected to this particular cardiologist. I asked her what she meant and she told me that he was ranked as one of the top cardiologists in the United States and that there was a waiting list to even get to see him. This was just another confirmation of the goodness of our God. After a couple more weeks of recovery, we resumed touring. I have to admit, the human side of me did get a little weary sometimes of carrying nitro pills and always wondering if the next chest pain was a heart attack or just reflux disease.

Our ministry kept growing, and many more stories were added to our collection. Some were great stories, while others were not good experiences. Still, God was blessing us in ways we had never anticipated. Many souls were being won to Christ, and many lives were touched in ways we will likely never know.

Each trip held a new adventure. We never knew what we would face when we pulled the motorhome out of the driveway, but we knew we were covered in prayer every time we left home. As a matter of fact, our next-door neighbor, Mrs. Salmon—whom I called "Mama Dot" because she was like a second mother to me—came out and climbed up into our motorhome every time we left. She would hold our hands, and she seemed to pray the heavens down. I always felt safe as long as she was praying for us.

Mama Dot would also point her finger at me with a stern, mother-like voice and say, "Just don't forget where you come from, young man. Don't go out there and get too big for your britches." We would drive away in tears every time she walked down out of the motorhome toward her house. It was a big loss to Esther and me when she passed away.

There were a few trips during which it was very obvious the hand of God was with us. Once, out in Colorado on our way back east, we got caught in a windstorm. We were driving eastward on the interstate, and there was a sixty-mph sustained wind blowing out of the south. The crosswind was so bad that there were trucks being blown over.

At one point, I saw a cloud of dust come out of nowhere. It looked like a dark brown cloud coming toward the highway. I had never experienced anything like that and wasn't sure what to do. I looked ahead and behind me to get an idea of where the traffic was. When

I hit the dust storm, the visibility went from clear to zero instantly. Here I was, driving a twelve-ton motorhome and towing a minivan. All I could do was take my foot off the accelerator and let it slow down, and pray.

I could barely even see the white lines and was using the rumble strips on the shoulder to stay on the road. Thankfully, it only lasted for about five minutes, but that was the longest five minutes I ever spent behind the wheel. That's when we decided it was time to park. We found an exit where there was a Walmart and pulled into the parking lot beside a big semi, using it as a shield against the wind. The storm lasted for hours. Finally, about 9:00 that night it began to subside so we started driving again. It was definitely a trip I will never forget.

Chapter 22

ALASKAN ADVENTURES

Yet another memorable trip happened after I met a gentleman from Alaska in Nashville during the Chet Atkins Convention. He said he enjoyed my music and asked me if I had ever considered touring in Alaska. I told him I had always dreamed of visiting there but did not have the connections to make it happen.

He asked if I would be interested in coming if he arranged the trip. My response was, of course! That very next year I found myself flying to Anchorage. He had arranged for me to minister in about six churches in the span of two weeks, along with a couple of fishing trips, which were a bonus.

I was a little nervous to fly alone and stay for two weeks with a family that I didn't know. The closer I got to the departure date, the more nervous I became. The very date that I was to fly out of Roanoke, I woke up with an intense fear about the trip. As Esther was driving me to the airport, I began to express my feelings to her, and I was having some chest discomfort because of it. She tried to encourage me, telling me that it was just stress and we would pray and everything would be okay. She let me off at the airport and we said our goodbyes.

As I sat at the gate waiting for the plane, I began to experience a panic attack like I had not experienced in more than thirty years. My heart was racing and my chest pains began to intensify. I reached in my pocket and discreetly took out a nitro pill and placed it under my tongue.

After a few minutes I could feel the rush of the nitro, but there was no change in the chest pain. I knew the enemy was trying to convince me through fear to cancel the trip and go home, and I was tempted to the extent that I tried to call Esther to have her come back and pick me up. She didn't answer for some reason, so after saying a prayer, I walked out on the tarmac and boarded the plane.

As we were taking off, I sat there praying and quoting the same Scripture that had sustained me so many times before. "For God has not given us the spirit of fear, but of power and of love and of a sound mind" (NKJV). Not only did I speak the Scripture quietly, I believed it. By the time the plane had leveled off I had been restored to a state of peace.

When we landed in Anchorage, the fear and anxiety were replaced with the excitement of what I knew God was going to do on this trip. I was picked up by my host and his wife at the airport. During the ride to their home, I discovered that they worked for Governor Sarah Palin as her personal mail screeners.

The first week of the trip went pretty well even though I was missing Esther a lot. Thankfully, I had a full schedule of concerts to keep me busy. I even played at a church that was attended by Sarah Palin's mother and had the honor of meeting her. Her name is Sally Heath, and she is such a kind and friendly lady. She invited us to her home that afternoon for coffee and cake. That's where I met her husband, Chuck. He was quite a character.

Chuck gave me a tour of his home and trophy room and I discovered we had something in common, because he loved to hunt and fish. In his room there were skins and mounts of Alaskan brown bear, white wolves, caribou, and moose. He was ready to share the story of every animal in his den. That evening's visit with Sarah's parents is one of my most special memories from that trip.

The second week, I was scheduled to drive down to Kenai and meet Pastor Wayne Coggins. In addition to being a pastor, he was a counselor and an author, as well as an experienced salmon fishing guide. I spent four nights with him and his wife, Marveen, in their home. They were very friendly and warm, and they went out of their way to make me feel welcome.

As kind as they were, I experienced another attack when I went to bed the first night in their home. Once again, my mind became my worst enemy and I began to feel lonely and afraid. I started thinking about how far away I was from a hospital and medical care and as I lay there, I began to feel chest pains again. It was about 2:00 in the morning and I was wide awake. My heart started beating faster and my mind was racing with worry.

I kept trying to tell myself that it was not a heart

attack; it was just anxiety and it was self-induced. For a little more self-assurance, I took an aspirin and a nitro pill, then just lay there on the bed. I started to pray, telling God, "I know I am not having a heart attack, and I will not wake up Pastor Wayne to take me to the hospital." I told Him that if I was going to die of a heart attack, it would be right there, because I was not going to move.

I began to speak 2 Timothy 1:7 over and over, and after what seemed like an hour, I found sleep. The next morning, I felt rested and grateful for that victory. I thanked God because with Him, I had just won another major battle. I was continually learning that the war with PTSD might not be over, but with each battle I faced, I could be victorious as long as I depended on His Word.

The rest of my Alaska trip proved to be a great time of ministry. Over the next three years, I would get to make two more ministry trips to Alaska, one of them with Esther. During that trip, Sarah Palin's parents, the Heaths, discovered I was in town. They happened to be celebrating their fiftieth wedding anniversary, and Sally called and invited me to come and play for their anniversary celebration. While Esther and I were there, we had the opportunity to meet Sarah Palin and her entire family. As well as experiencing God's mercy and comforting power, often we would experience His favor. Even now, I thank Him for that daily.

Chapter 23

PUT ON THE ARMOR OF GOD

Along this life journey, God has taught me to trust Him more and more. While there have been many moments of joy, at other times I have found myself helpless and in need of God's reassurance.

One such time was when I was traveling on a three-week tour with a dear friend, Jimmy Davis, who was a singing evangelist. During this particular trip, I was scheduled to play in New Jersey with the great Les Paul. It was going to be one of the major events of my ministry career. I was a little nervous, but so excited that I would not only get to meet but actually perform with one of my guitar heroes and one of the greatest music legends of all time.

My motorhome was parked at a family friend's home in northern Maryland, and a week before I was scheduled to drive to New Jersey, I began to feel chest pains again, as well as severe fatigue. After a lot of convincing, my friends took me to the emergency room in Bel Air, Maryland. I was immediately rushed into a room and within minutes, the doctor came to see me. He said, "Mr. Kiser, you are having a heart attack. Please try not to move; we are going to take care of you."

As I was waiting to be moved into the catheterization lab, I felt that empty, lonely feeling again. My good friends were there, but my wife was not with me. My friends prayed for me as I fought back the tears and tried to pretend to be brave. Deep inside, I was scared to death. Thankfully, it wasn't too long before God sent a feeling of peace and security that everything was going to be alright.

During the procedure, they found two blockages and placed two stents in my heart. I was sent home and grounded for a month to recover. Needless to say, along with the frustration of another heart issue, I was disappointed that I would not get to meet Les Paul. A few weeks later, around the time I was released from the doctor and could resume my music ministry, Les passed away.

Often it seems that the big plans we make for our lives don't turn out quite as we expected or hoped. I am reminded constantly that it takes as much faith to accept the struggles that life hands us as it does to believe that God will see us through these struggles. As Hebrews 11:1 reminds us, "Now faith is the substance of things hoped for, the evidence of things not seen" (KJV).

Over the next few years, I experienced two more major surgeries. One of them was a spinal fusion in which plates and screws were placed in my lower back to fuse my L4 and L5 vertebrae. Again, I experienced a definite move and answer from God.

I had wrestled with the decision to have this surgery for months, even though I was experiencing constant severe pain. I just didn't want to go through another surgery and long recovery period. I made the mistake of asking too many people what I should do, and of course every person had an opinion. Some were yes, some were no. Thankfully, I received a clear answer a few days before the operation was to take place.

It was Thursday, and my surgery was scheduled for the following Tuesday. I was so tired of not feeling 100 percent committed to having the operation. When I got up that Thursday morning, I prayed and asked God to give me an answer that day that would leave me with no doubt.

That afternoon, I was watching the 5:00 local news as Esther prepared supper upstairs. A commercial came on for the LewisGale Medical Center there in Virginia, saying that it featured one of the top orthopedic surgery centers in the eastern part of the country. The surgeon who appeared onscreen performing a procedure was my surgeon! I had never seen that commercial before that day and have never seen it since, but I knew it was God's way of speaking to this hard-headed guitar player and answering my prayer.

The procedure went without a problem and for the first time in over fifteen years, my leg was no longer numb and the lower back pain was gone. God's faithfulness had prevailed!

Our minds can play tricks on us, and there have been days when my only alternative was to just "suck it up" and go on no matter how I was feeling. One of these times was during a ministry trip to Colorado. We were on our way, and I was feeling fine physically. The problem was that about halfway there, I started to feel that awful separation anxiety. There was no reason that I could identify; I just started feeling uneasy and uncomfortable. The more I thought about it, the sicker I began to feel. I started thinking about cancelling the tour and going back home. The main reason I pressed on was that one of the scheduled concerts was a ticketed event, and I did not want to cancel and put a burden on the person who had arranged it.

We arrived in Colorado, and for the entire week it seemed that all I wanted to do was sleep. I had no energy and no desire to go anywhere, but I felt that my only choice was to push on and do the best I could. In time, I began to feel normal again.

The truth is, if Satan can find even a small opening in our armor, or if we choose to leave off just a portion of our armor, then that opening is where he will target to destroy us. God's Word tells us to "Put on the whole armor of God that you may be able to stand against the wiles of the devil" (Ephesians 6:11 NKJV). The bottom line is that sometimes we have to press on no matter how we feel. That's when faith is exercised. Like the human body, the more we exercise, the stronger we become.

There are times, however, that we are blessed to see the full glory of God and His goodness. These are the special times that seem to renew and increase our faith and trust in Him.

A good example of this was during one of my Alaskan trips when I met Dwayne King of Kingdom Air Corps. Mr. King has a ministry of training young pilots who aspire to be missionaries to become bush pilots. These young pilots learn to land on grass strips, dry stony riverbeds, and snow. He also teaches them to work on their own aircraft, which is important on the mission field, where no mechanics are likely to be found.

Mr. King gave me a tour all around the Kingdom facility, the dorms, and the chapel. He told me of how God had used him to win souls in Russia and provided for his ministry to grow. All of the planes on his campus were donated, repaired, and certified to be air-worthy. He also took us on a plane ride over some of the Alaskan glaciers and snow-capped mountains. I have to admit, I was a little nervous when we started picking up speed on that grassy runway that was shaved off the top of a mountain.

At the end of the runway there was a 4000-foot drop-off, straight down. Of course, we were in the air well before we reached the drop-off, but it was still pretty exciting. That wasn't a spirit of fear, it was just being human. At one time we were cruising just below the mountain ridges. As far as the eye could see, there was nothing but gigantic snow-capped mountains and miles and miles of beautiful glaciers.

Out of the silence, Dwayne began to sing through his intercom into our headphones, "Then sings my soul, my Savior God to Thee, how great Thou art, how great

Thou art...." Tears welled up in my eyes as I was awed by God's majestic creation. Many times when we get to slow down and just experience God's beautiful world as He intended, our faith is increased simply because we see His mighty handiwork.

Chapter 24
TRUST IN ALL THINGS

It was the winter of 2013, and we were preparing to make our annual trip to Florida for three months of concerts. For many years, God had blessed us with a full schedule every winter in Florida. Our motorhome was packed and ready to go. I decided to go to the back yard and check my shed to make sure it was locked. As always, I was probably in a bit of a rush and not being as careful as I should have been.

I was hurrying down the cinder block steps, not knowing the bottom step was wet and mossy. When my foot hit the step, I slipped, and both feet went out from under me. I landed backwards on my left shoulder, and the impact was excruciating. I felt like my arm was broken and I immediately had a sickening feeling along with the pain. My wife drove me to the emergency room and after an examination and X-rays, the doctor told me it was not broken but that I should have it checked by an orthopedic surgeon. The way my shoulder was hurting, I began to realize that this could be serious.

When we got back home I made an appointment with an orthopedic surgeon and made a few phone calls to adjust my concert schedule. After the surgeon examined me, he warned me that this could be a serious rotator cuff injury. I guess my stubborn side took over, and I told him I would take my chances and try to do my tour.

He smiled, looked at Esther, and quietly said, "He'll be back." Within a few days we were on our way to Florida just a week later than we planned. I placed a pillow on the left control panel of the motorhome to rest my left arm and with some Advil, made the 700-mile drive to Florida. That winter, I played forty concerts in twelve weeks with a lot of pain.

After talking with a close friend who was a physician's assistant to an orthopedic surgeon, I faced the reality that I probably had some major rotator cuff damage. While trying to "man up," so to speak, to make my commitments, I was making the situation worse. With the help of a lot of ibuprofen, heating pads, and ice packs, we were able to complete the concert tour.

As soon as I got home, I made an appointment to see the surgeon, and he scheduled an MRI. After it was done, he called me in and said the news was not good. He informed me that there was major damage to the rotator cuff and that one tendon was detached. The only hope of repairing the shoulder would be for me to undergo surgery. The recovery time would likely be at least eight weeks, and I would spend much of that time having intense physical therapy.

We scheduled a time to have my shoulder repaired, and during the drive home from the doctor's office, for the first time, I began to weep. The tears were not from pain; they were from frustration. I began to pray, and my prayer was not one of submission. It was more a prayer of anger at God. It was pretty much, "What did I do to deserve this? I mean, after all, God, I have been working for you. How could you let this happen?"

I admit, I was almost ashamed of my prayer. Sometimes as Christians we can have a feeling of entitlement, especially when we are working for Him in ministry. We feel that if we are living and working for Him, we should be exempt from problems and pain. Thank God we serve a Father who allows us to be human and have human emotions.

I was sitting in a church parking lot near my home, praying and crying, because I didn't want Esther to see me like this. There were so many emotions that were rushing through my head. I felt guilt, thinking that if I'd had it repaired right away, it wouldn't be as severe. I was worried thinking, how can we go for eight to ten weeks with no income? I felt upset with God as well as with myself.

After sitting there in my car alone for a while, I began to calm down. I know it was His Holy Spirit that began to give me comfort and gently remind me that I had gone through many hard trials in my life. He had brought me through every one of them, so why should this one be any different?

I finally dried my tears and drove home to break the news to Esther. As I've gone through rough times like that, I have often stopped to thank God that I married such an amazing prayer warrior and a woman of faith. She was much more concerned about my pain and what

I would be going through physically than how we would pay bills. The financial part was the least of her concerns. She knew God would see us through, as He had always done in the past.

The day of the surgery arrived and as always, I lay in bed the night before thinking about "what ifs." What if the surgeon can't repair my shoulder? What if he makes a mistake and I am never able to play guitar again? This was another manifestation of "the spirit of fear." As I tried to get to sleep, I quoted 2 Timothy 1:7 again. After a while, I drifted off to sleep.

When the surgery was over and I was in the recovery room, the surgeon came in to talk with me. He said he felt good about the repair but that it would be a long, slow recovery, and if I wanted to gain full use of my shoulder I would need to follow his instructions exactly. The surgery was so intense that he wouldn't even let me begin physical therapy for six weeks. I had to wear a sling and sleep in a recliner for the next two months. To add insult to injury, I am left-handed, so Esther had to help me do everything.

I remember her getting emotional only one time during this ordeal. One night while I was sitting there watching TV, the fingers of my left hand just felt like they needed to be on the fingerboard of my guitar. I asked Esther to uncase one of my lightest acoustic guitars and hand it to me. I laid the guitar against my chest so I wouldn't have to move my arm or shoulder in the sling and tried to place my hand around the neck of the guitar.

When I wrapped my fingers around it and tried to form a chord, the pain went all the way up my arm. I had tears in my eyes, and I knew it was too soon. Esther saw the hurt and disappointment on my face and tried, unsuccessfully, to hide her own tears. She put the guitar back on the stand, and I just had to accept the fact that I was not ready.

In a few weeks I started physical therapy. My therapist was a nice guy, but I jokingly called him my "physical terrorist" for obvious reasons. Because my arm had been in a sling for six weeks, my shoulder was what they called "frozen." That meant when he removed the sling, my arm and shoulder still wouldn't move.

The first day he said, "I'm sorry for what I have to do," and he gently took my arm and started stretching it. I thought it was going to snap like a rubber band, and I began to break out in a sweat. After a few days of therapy, to my surprise, the muscle began to stretch and move. It was still going to be a long, slow process, but I was willing to endure anything to get back to playing my guitar. After a few more weeks, I began to try to play. It felt like I was learning all over again, and it was a very emotional time.

Just about the time I was beginning to think everything was going to work out, I began to have chest pains again during my daily walks. After a visit with my cardiologist, he scheduled another heart catheterization. He found another blocked artery and put in another stent. I knew then that even with physical therapy, I would be recovering for another few weeks. I began to get very frustrated and was fighting anger once again.

A couple weeks after the heart procedure, as I was sitting at home watching TV with Esther, I got a phone call. I was feeling pretty sorry for myself even though during this entire ordeal, somehow money seemed to come in and our bills were being paid. Even though God was being faithful and sustaining us, I was still fighting an attitude. On the phone was a friend of mine from Florida named Russell. He said, "Hey brother, I know you have been going through a lot lately and I just wanted to call to let you know I have been thinking about you and praying for you."

After we chatted for a few minutes, Russell asked if he could pray with me. We had a time of prayer, then said our goodbyes. After we hung up, I sat there and began to cry. Russell had only been out of the hospital for a few weeks himself. The difference was that he had been in and out of the hospital for nearly five years and was sent home under hospice care, yet he called to cheer me up. After the tears passed, I began to ask God to forgive me for being such a whiny baby. I realized that even though I was having problems, there were certainly other people in the world who were suffering a lot more. After all, we never had to miss a meal, all of our bills were paid, and my body was healing, albeit slower than I had hoped for. God's Word says, "Beloved, think it not strange concerning the fiery trial which is to try you, as though some strange thing happened unto you: but rejoice, inasmuch as ye are partakers of Christ's sufferings; that, when His glory shall be revealed, ye may be glad also with exceeding joy" (1 Peter 4:12–13 KJV).

God always sees us through these tough times. With a lot of prayer and a lot of therapy and determination, not to mention hours of practice on the guitar, within a few more weeks I was able to resume playing my guitar and ministering. The biggest difference was that I now had a refreshed message of God's goodness and faithfulness.

Chapter 25
MOVING FORWARD

There were also times that God protected us from certain danger, when we were totally dependent on His mercy and goodness. Once while on tour in Colorado, we were parked at a church where I was scheduled for a concert. While we were there, Colorado experienced one of the most devastating floods in history. Every night for almost a week we were watching the news of devastation and even death.

We were parked next to a building on the church property and we had backed down just off the pavement. One Wednesday night, it was raining so hard that it was difficult to hear the TV in the motorhome. It had rained like that all day long and into the night.

I decided to go ahead and try and move the motorhome, even though there was no river or stream within a mile of us. I soon discovered that the coach was stuck in the mud and was not going anywhere. I decided that I had to find some way to move it, so I called a friend who owned a trucking company. He promised me that he would have his tow truck out there by 9:30 the next morning. The rain was so loud it was hard to sleep.

Just before 9:00 the next morning, I was standing in the doorway of the motorhome, drinking coffee and watching the rain. All of a sudden, out of nowhere I saw a river coming toward us. I didn't even have time to panic—it was instant survival mode. I told Esther to get ready because we were going to have to get out of here.

I ran outside and moved our car to the highest location on the lot and by the time I got back to the coach, the water was around a foot deep and still rising rapidly. The pastor came out of the church, and I told him we needed to get Esther out of the coach. By now, the water was almost up to the door.

There were also some men there who had been re-paving the church parking lot before the rains came. They were there that morning to move their paving equipment. The pastor told one of the pavers about my wife being trapped in the motorhome, and he drove the large paving machine through the water to the door of the coach. We helped Esther out of the coach but when she stepped onto the ground, the water was so deep and swift that she couldn't walk without us half-carrying her to the paving machine, which was only a few feet away.

I have fished for trout in swift waters and this was just as swift, but the difference was that this water was full of debris. The only humor in the ordeal was that as I was trying to walk back to higher ground after Esther was rescued, I saw little prairie dogs swimming by, looking up at me as if to say, "What in the world is going on?" Even in the midst of that nightmarish ordeal, I had to laugh.

About the time Esther was rescued, the tow truck driver arrived. I told him, "It's too late; it can't be pulled out now." He looked at the situation and told me if I could get the cable hooked to the back of the coach, he could still pull it out. I didn't believe it, but Pastor Jim and I walked through the floodwater to the back of the coach, reached down into that cold, muddy water, and hooked his cable to the hitch on the back of the motorhome.

My friend then told me to go inside the motorhome, start it, release the brake, and put it in reverse. I looked at him like he was crazy, and he laughed and said, "It's a diesel, it will start—just do it." I climbed up into the coach and sure enough, it started. I put it in reverse and to my total surprise, he was able to pull me onto the high part of the driveway.

After we all thanked God for helping us through this, it dawned on me that if this had happened about three hours earlier, Esther and I would have been asleep. The motorhome could have been swept around the side of the building, and the end result could have been a disaster. I'm sure there are many other times throughout our lives that God has spared us from disaster when we were not even aware. That's the kind of God we serve.

We were able to drive the motorhome to a safer place where we were away from the floodwaters, and we stayed there for another two days while it rained. After the rain finally stopped, I tried to assess the damage. All of the basement storage area was full of mud and water, and we lost $2,000 worth of CDs. I spent two days washing mud out of the basement area and trying to dry it out. I had thrown all of my sound equipment and electronics into the motorhome during the flooding, and thankfully, everything but the CDs seemed okay.

After arriving back in Virginia, we discovered that we had sustained much more damage than first thought. Thank God for good insurance, because it covered most of the damage, which included a diesel generator.

In spite of the trials and frustrations my family and I have experienced, God has blessed me with His favor so many undeserved times. I have seen Him move in miraculous ways throughout this ministry. I have had opportunities to experience special things in my life that without God's favor, I don't think I would ever have experienced.

Esther always told me I had too many interests and hobbies. I'm not sure that's possible, but she is probably right. I have loved cars and drag racing since I was a kid. Because of friends I've met through the music ministry, I got to sit in a 2,000-horsepower, top-fuel dragster while they started the engine, which was a thrill. I also love scuba diving, and through another friend I met while touring, I was invited to swim with and bottle-feed a pygmy sperm whale which was in captivity at a marine hospital. During my ministry, there have been so many special things that God has allowed me to experience— not because I deserve His favor, but because we serve a great God.

It has now been more than forty years since that fateful day when the hunting accident changed my life forever. At this point, it seems almost like a story, or something that was experienced in another life. In one way, I can remember it in great detail, but in another way, it feels like it happened to someone else.

I am still so thankful that God spared my life on that day. I am also glad that He has allowed me to share my story and try to render hope to people whose lives seem hopeless. The older we get, the more we learn that life is a continual lesson—and a gift. We share what we can, and we draw from the experiences of others when we get a chance.

I could not understand decades ago why God would allow something like that accident to happen. Now when I look back, I see how He has used this story to give encouragement to so many people. Being a veteran myself, I have always had a special place in my heart for our veterans. No one can imagine many of the things our warriors have experienced, and I certainly don't pretend to understand what someone else has been through.

The Bible tells us, "Be sober, be vigilant; because your adversary the devil, as a roaring lion, walketh about, seeking whom he may devour" (1 Peter 5:8 KJV). When the enemy is seeking to destroy someone's soul, their mind is often the first target. That's why so many who are plagued by fear try drugs and alcohol to alter their state of mind. But that approach never solves the original problem and only adds more problems.

I have spoken to many veterans who were suffering from PTSD. Almost all of them tried numbing the pain with drugs or alcohol, yet not one of them could say it worked. Let me emphasize here that I am neither a doctor nor a psychologist. I am simply a man who understands the horror of a violent, nearly fatal experience from a gunshot. I have gone through the aftermath of panic attacks and nightmares. I know what it feels like, and I know they are not a measure of a man's strength.

We can deny it or try to rationalize it, but for me the true giver of peace is the only one who can give back peace of mind. This brings me back to the verse that has been my saving grace during some of the darkest days of my life—2 Timothy 1:7: "For God has not given us a spirit of fear, but of power and of love and of a sound mind" (NKJV).

Though your struggles may be different from mine, I hope my story has offered some encouragement. I don't know everything, but this I know for sure: If you put your life in God's hands and stand on His Word, He has promised that He will never leave you nor forsake you. No matter what you go through, He offers strength to sustain you. May God bless and keep you along your journey.

Guitars for Vets® (G4V)

G4V was founded in 2007 by guitar instructor, Patrick Nettesheim and his student, Vietnam era Marine, Dan Van Buskirk.

The men realized that the guitar and lessons were a catalyst for positive human interaction and joy where it had once been lost.

Guitars and lessons are provided at no cost to US Military Veterans who are referred by their case/social worker at The Department of Veterans Affairs facilities.

Ten private lessons are provided using practice guitars donated by the local community.

Upon completion, the Vet/student is awarded a new acoustic guitar and accessories.

The Veterans continue this journey as long as they desire with ongoing group lessons.

Playing guitar brings joy and opens up "windows of serenity" - it is meditation in motion.

Though not a cure or treatment (we are not therapists) for PTSD and other injuries, the G4V program provides a positive, rewarding step on the Veterans' journey toward peace and happiness.

G4V is implemented by hundreds of volunteers at more than 80 Chapters and 40 States Nationwide.

Over 3,000 guitars and 30,000 lessons have been given to service men and women who suffer from trauma related to their military experience.

It costs only $200.00 to enroll a Veteran in the G4V program.

This curriculum is supported by donations of instruments and funds.

"I ask all of you who feel that you have benefitted from the sacrifices of our brothers and sisters in the Armed Forces to join our mission."

Guitars for Vets is a 501(c)3 non-profit organization and your donations may be tax deductible.

Please go to www.Guitars4Vets.org or call 855-G4V-HERO to donate and make a difference.

"You have the opportunity to enrich the lives of those who would lay down theirs for us."

You can put "the healing power of music in the hands of heroes™."